STAND
on the
WORD
Study Guide

PAUL'S LETTERS TO LEADERS

1 TIMOTHY
TITUS
2 TIMOTHY

A 7-Day Journey through the Word
with Tony Perkins

FAMILY RESEARCH COUNCIL
SINCE 1983

FIDELIS PUBLISHING ®

ISBN: 9798999024664

Paul's Letters to Leaders: 1 Timothy, Titus, 2 Timothy
A Stand on the Word Study Guide

Content contributor: Dr. Kenyn Cureton
Cover design: Diana Lawrence
Copyediting and interior typesetting: Lisa Parnell

Order at www.faithfultext.com for a significant discount. Email info@fidelis publishing.com to inquire about bulk purchase discounts.

Fidelis Publishing, LLC Sterling, VA • Nashville, TN www.fidelispublishing.com

Manufactured in the United States of America

10 9 8 7 6 5 4 3 2 1

Contents

— Day 1 —

Paul's Letters to Leaders: An Introduction

Welcome to the Stand on the Word Study Guide to the Pastoral Letters: 1 Timothy, 2 Timothy, and Titus. Paul's letters to leaders hold a unique place in the New Testament. They differ from Paul's other letters not only in their subject matter but also in their personal tone. Rather than addressing entire congregations, these letters are directed to two individual leaders: Timothy, whom Paul referred to as his "true son in the faith" and indeed "a beloved son" (1 Tim. 1:2; 2 Tim. 1:2), and Titus, "a true son in our common faith" (Titus 1:4). In these letters, we see Paul's heart as a mentor, pastor, and spiritual father, concerned not only for doctrinal faithfulness in the churches but also for the flourishing of these two men as leaders.

Paul's Relationship with Timothy

We are introduced to Timothy in Acts 16 during Paul's second missionary journey through Lystra and Derbe in Lyconia, the southwestern part of Roman Galatia. Timothy was the son of a believing Jewish mother and a Greek father (Acts 16:1). As we see in Paul's second letter, Timothy's mother Eunice and grandmother Lois taught him the Scriptures from an early age and they apparently came to faith in Christ (2 Tim. 1:5; 3:15). Timothy may have also responded to the gospel when Paul came through their area on his first missionary journey. When Paul made the return trip, he heard about Timothy. Luke reports, "He was well spoken of by the brethren who were at Lystra and Iconium" (Acts 16:2). Consequently, "Paul wanted to have him go on with him" (v. 3a). Since Timothy's father was a Greek, Paul had Timothy circumcised so that his participation would not be a stumbling block to any of the Jews they would try to reach together (v. 3b). From that point forward, Timothy became one of Paul's closest companions and most trusted co-laborers.

We see the depth of their bond in multiple passages. In Philippians 2:19–22, Paul commends Timothy's unique character: "For I have no one like-minded, who will sincerely care for your state . . . that as a son with his father he served with me in the gospel." This description highlights Timothy's loyalty, humility, and shared heart for Christ's mission. Timothy also appears as co-sender in several of Paul's letters (e.g., 2 Corinthians, Philippians, Colossians, 1–2 Thessalonians, Philemon), which underscores his active involvement in ministry and Paul's complete trust in him. By the time Paul writes these Pastoral Epistles, Timothy has become the key leader in Ephesus, tasked with shepherding the church there, ordaining leaders, and combating false teaching (1 Tim. 1:3–4). Paul writes to encourage, instruct, and strengthen this younger leader, reminding him not to neglect the gift he had received (1 Tim. 4:14), to "fight the good fight of faith" (1 Tim. 6:12), and to "endure hardship" like a soldier of Christ (2 Tim. 2:3). Paul tasked Timothy with ordaining bishops and deacons in the house churches throughout Ephesus (see 1 Tim. 3:1–13).

Paul's Relationship with Titus

Unlike Paul's specific encounter with Timothy related in Acts, the exact location and date of Paul's connection with Titus are unknown, although the meeting likely took place before AD 47 (see Acts 11:29–30). Referring to that time, Paul says in Galatians 2:1, "Then after fourteen years I went up again to Jerusalem with Barnabas, and also took Titus with me." Since Paul referred to Titus as his "true son in our common faith" (Titus 1:4), he was likely won to faith in Christ by Paul. Also, unlike Timothy, Titus was a purely Gentile convert (Gal. 2:3), which seems to be the reason Paul brought him along as he ministered to Gentiles, as proof that God indeed saves non-Jewish people, and that they could be fully accepted by God without circumcision. Titus traveled with Paul extensively. Paul trusted him to handle sensitive issues in the difficult church at Corinth (2 Cor. 7:6–16), and Paul praised him as his "partner and fellow worker" (2 Cor. 8:23). One of Paul's ministry patterns that we see in Acts is that he "appointed elders in every church" (Acts 14:23a). Paul must have mentored Titus to prepare him to do the same, since he writes, "For this reason I left you in Crete, that you should set in order the things that are lacking, and appoint elders in every city as I commanded you" (Titus 1:5). This responsibility shows Paul's confidence in Titus's maturity and leadership.

Setting for the Pastoral Epistles

It is apparent that the letters to these two young leaders were written near the end of Paul's ministry. Strong biblical evidence and tradition place the writing of 1 Timothy and Titus after Paul's release from his first Roman imprisonment, which apparently happened after what Luke records in Acts 28. In 2 Timothy 4:16–17, Paul references his "first defense" or trial and indicates that the matter ended favorably: "I was delivered out of the mouth of the lion," apparently referring to his release. These clues point to at least two imprisonments for Paul in Rome. In fact, there is evidence we can piece together from these letters to Timothy and Titus that suggest Paul embarked on a fourth missionary journey upon his release from this first imprisonment. Specifically, Paul tells us that he visited Troas (v. 13) and Miletus (v. 20). He was *en route* for Macedonia, thus his instructions for Timothy to stay put in Ephesus (see 1 Tim. 1:3). Yet there is no firm evidence that Paul ever made it to Ephesus to visit Timothy. However, Paul may have visited Titus in Crete, but that is conjecture.

It was also during this time that church tradition alleges Paul made it all the way to Spain. Only three decades after Paul's martyrdom, Clement, the bishop of Rome, wrote around AD 95 that Paul "having taught righteousness unto the whole world and having reached the farthest bounds of the West; and when he had borne his testimony before the rulers, so he departed from the world and went unto the holy place . . ." (see 1 Clement 5.6). For a contemporary Roman, the "farthest bounds of the West" usually meant Spain but could actually refer to Gaul or even the British Isles. Regardless, we have sufficient biblical evidence that Paul was active in Macedonia and Greece between his release and his re-arrest. Some scholars suggest he was arrested in the western districts of Macedonia or Epirus.[1] He had planned to winter in Nicopolis (Titus 3:12) and that may have been where he was apprehended and then transported back to Rome, imprisoned, and awaited execution. We don't know for sure. What we do know is that 2 Timothy was written during Paul's second imprisonment shortly before his death, which Paul characterizes as imminent (see 4:6–8). The above circumstances situate the Pastoral Epistles firmly in the final chapter of Paul's incredible life and ministry, when he was keenly aware of his need to pass the torch of leadership to the next generation who would succeed him. This study guide will explore Paul's letters to these young leaders.

How to Get the Most from the Study Guide

While the study guide offers spiritual insights and applications, the real impact comes from the words of Scripture, which is the Word of God. Please read the selected text for the day in your own Bible. God's Word is "living and powerful" (Heb. 4:12). The Spirit of God uses His Word to change your life. Nothing else can do that. So before reading the daily commentary, read God's Word!

In fact, here are five habits to cultivate as you approach God's Word each day:

1. *Read it through:* Don't skip around. Read the entire selection of Scripture. If you are pressed for time, please read the Bible before you read the study guide notes. So read it through.
2. *Think it over:* Meditate on it. Let it marinate in your mind. If you can, take notes. We provide a notes page at the end of each day. Think it over.
3. *Pray it in:* Personalize the Scripture. Turn the verse that speaks to you into a prayer and then pray it into your life. Ask God what you need to do in response. This leads to the next habit.
4. *Live it out:* Consider ways to apply what God is revealing to you and ways you can obey Him. Put His Word into

practice. Make it a part of who you are, how you think, how you speak, and how you behave toward God and other people. In other words, take God's Word and live it out.

5. *Pass it on:* Don't keep it to yourself. People are in your life who need the same truth God has spoken to you in His Word. Share it. Pass it on.

About Stand on the Word

Stand on the Word is a ministry of Family Research Council, whose mission is to serve in the kingdom of God by championing faith, family, and freedom in public policy and in the culture from a biblical worldview. The purpose of Stand on the Word is to lay the foundation for a biblical worldview through daily reading and application of God's Word. For the daily journey, we have created a chronologically prioritized reading plan through the entire Bible that can be accessed at frc.org/Bible, by texting the word *Bible* to 67742, or by downloading the Stand Firm app.

Ephesus

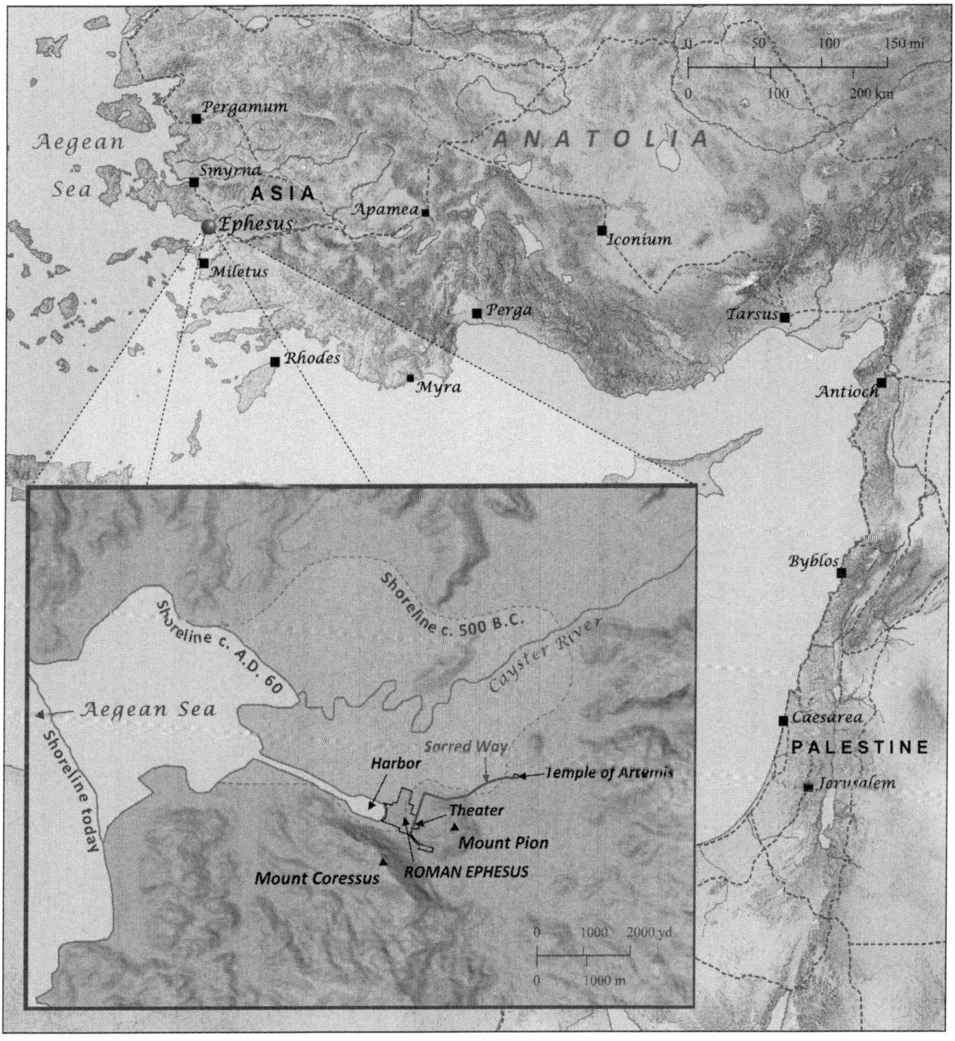

0
50
100
150 mi
0
100
200 km
Pergamum
Aegean
Sea
Smyrna
ASIA
ANATOLIA
Apamea
Ephesus
Iconium
Miletus
Perga
Tarsus
Rhodes
Myra
Antioch
Byblos
Shoreline c. 500 B.C.
Shoreline c. A.D. 60
Cayster River
Aegean Sea
Shoreline today
Sacred Way
Harbor
Temple of Artemis
Theater
Mount Pion
Mount Coressus
ROMAN EPHESUS
0
1000
2000 yd
0
1000 m
Caesarea
PALESTINE
Jerusalem

— Day 2 —

Today's Reading: 1 Timothy 1–2

Verse of the Day

> Therefore I exhort first of all that supplications, prayers, intercessions, and giving of thanks be made for all men, for kings and all who are in authority, that we may lead a quiet and peaceable life in all godliness and reverence.
>
> *— 1 Timothy 2:1–2*

Please read the entire Scripture selection in your own Bible and highlight or underline verses that stand out to you before you read the observations and engage the questions below.

Today, we begin the first of three pastoral epistles as we read 1 Timothy 1–2. Our key verses are 1 Timothy 2:1–2: "Therefore I exhort first of all that supplications, prayers, intercessions, and giving of thanks be made for all men, for kings and all who are in authority, that we may lead a quiet and peaceable life in all godliness and reverence." Why should we pray for government leaders? Does it make any difference? I can tell you from personal experience, it does indeed make a difference. I could share example after example of answered prayer where I saw the fulfillment of Proverbs 21:1: "The king's heart is in the hand of the LORD, like the rivers of water; He turns it wherever He wishes." When God answers our petitions for a government leader or a policy, it reveals the power of prayer and serves as a reminder of why we should pray.

With almost all these passages, there are many biblical truths to consider and contemplate that cannot be fully unpacked in a brief devotional. However, I hope that you read these chapters thoroughly, meditate upon them, and consider the truths that you come across in these two chapters. Beginning in 1 Timothy 1:2 we read, "To Timothy, a true son in the faith: Grace, mercy, and peace from God our Father and Jesus Christ our Lord." Although not central to the message, it's worth noting what Paul did in the opening of his letter. Paul was releasing a blessing and an affirmation over Timothy. We need to realize the power of our words and what we speak, whether to build up and encourage (as we're often instructed in Scripture to be careful about what we say) or whether our words are being used to tear down and destroy.

Again, Paul is writing this letter from somewhere in Macedonia, as he notes in verses 3–4: "I urged you when I went into Macedonia—remain at Ephesus that you may charge some that they teach no other doctrine, nor give heed to fables and endless genealogies, which cause disputes rather than godly edification which is in faith." Preaching the truth of God's Word is essential to the health and well-being of a local body of believers. When Paul was on his way to Jerusalem, he stopped and visited with the leaders of Ephesus, recorded in Acts 20, and warned them to be on guard against false teachers. Even then, Paul called those false teachers "savage wolves" (v. 29).

It is helpful to have a better understanding of the context of these instructions from Paul. The church was not like it is today, where people from around the community gather in a particular designated church building with a particular name. In the first century, there were no "churches" like we have today. Church buildings really didn't appear until the early third century. Prior to that time, believers mostly met in homes. Ephesus had one of the largest Christian populations in the first century. That meant there were a number of homes they met in; they didn't meet in just one. Therefore, there were probably scores of house churches, meaning there were scores of pastors and church leaders that Timothy had to oversee.

Also keep in mind, these pastors were not graduates of some seminary. They were discipled and mentored, but then it was on-the-job training. Remember, they had only the Old Testament, maybe Matthew's Gospel, along with a few letters from Paul and that of James. You can see how easily it would have been for a "wolf" to sneak into the sheepfold and to start teaching some wild idea. That's why it is so important for us to focus on the revealed truth of God, not some hidden truth that requires a spiritual "decoder ring" to decipher. We waste precious time pursuing the latest "hot take" from some so-called "teacher" and their beliefs that are not clearly rooted in Scripture. Focus on what is clearly there in the Bible that edifies and builds up, rather than that which leads to endless disputes. Don't misunderstand; it is great to have a dialogue. I enjoy conversations with my friends who are Bible scholars and theologians, discussing topics of interest and debate. Yet at the end of the day, the local church needs to focus on the basics of sharing the simple but powerful gospel and teaching the straightforward principles of the revealed Word of God, which should result in mature and multiplying disciples of Jesus.

Paul also addresses the purpose of the Mosaic Law. Notice in 1 Timothy 1:5–7: "Now the purpose of the commandment is love from a pure heart, from a good conscience, and from sincere faith, from which some, having strayed, have turned aside to idle talk, desiring to be teachers of the law, understanding neither what they say nor the things which they affirm." In other words, there were so-called "teachers," who apparently took too much pride in pushing people back to the law. In the south, we talk about those who "put on airs." Yet Paul said they had no right to be prideful because they didn't know what they were talking about. Paul points out that the purpose of the commandment for the believer is to inspire us to "love from a pure heart." In verses 8–11, Paul talks about the purpose of the law for those who are outside the faith. The law merely convicts of sin and threatens penalties for breaking it, and thus restrains evil. It is not there to build up and to edify like the gospel of Jesus Christ does.

In verses 12–14, Paul thanks God, acknowledging that Christ appointed him to ministry despite his sinful and rebellious past. He was once "a blasphemer, a persecutor, and an insolent man." Yet God's mercy and grace not only forgave him but also empowered him. What a great reminder that our past and indeed our present is not too broken for God's transforming grace! Paul offers as proof what we might call the "Gospel in a Sentence" in verse 15: "This is a faithful saying and worthy of all acceptance, that Christ Jesus came into the world to save sinners, of whom I am chief." Note he didn't put that in the past tense but the present. Yet here's the point: If God could save the persecutor Saul and transform him into the apostle Paul, God can save anyone! Paul is an example of God's amazing grace. That loved one you've been praying for who is lost and far away from God? Keep on praying because nothing is impossible with God! The gospel is not about who we are and what we've done but about who Christ is and what He has done. Christ came to save us sinners. That is why He is worthy of our praise (v. 17)!

Now let's drop down to verse 18: "This charge I commit to you, son Timothy, according to the prophecies previously made concerning you, that by them you may wage the good warfare." Talk about being politically incorrect, Paul directs: "Wage the good warfare." Following Jesus is a call to warfare. Yes, spiritual warfare but warfare nonetheless, and we're to fight it. We're to fight it with all that we have. Do not be a deserter or a deconstructionist of your faith, like Hymenaeus or Alexander, whom we read about in verse 19: "having faith and a good conscience, which some having rejected, concerning the faith have suffered shipwreck." If you depart from the faith, depart from the truth of God's word, and you will end up a wreck. Paul says, "of whom are Hymenaeus and Alexander, whom I delivered to Satan that they may learn not to blaspheme."

Next, let's move on to chapter 2, where we see the other priorities that Paul talks about for the local church: "Therefore I exhort first of all that supplications, prayers, intercessions, and giving of thanks be made for all men, for kings and all who are in authority, that we may lead a quiet and peaceable life in all godliness and reverence. For this is good and acceptable in the sight of God our Savior, who desires all men to be saved and to come to the knowledge of the truth" (2:1–4).

Let us unpack this important teaching about prayer. Paul tells Timothy, his young protégé, that prayer is the first order of business for the church. After ensuring that the doctrine is correct, it is clear that Paul believes the church should concern itself with government and government leaders. That may cause some folk spiritual whiplash because we've been told to keep God out of government and faith out of public life. Yet, that is not what the Bible instructs us here. So what is the church to do? First of all, make supplications. That's a request—recognizing the pressing and present need and the inability to meet those needs in and of ourselves. Basically, it's a recognition that we need God's help and our leaders need God's help. Paul speaks of prayers. That is a devotion and commitment. Then he speaks of intercessions. Coming to God, drawing close to Him on behalf of others. We're lifting them up before the Lord. We're praying for them. This is what we're supposed to do for government leaders.

Some might ask, "Do we only pray for the good ones or the ones we agree with?" No, Paul directs us to pray for all of them. That is somewhat surprising given the identity of Caesar at this time: Nero. Therefore, Paul is saying we should even pray for a wicked ruler like Nero. In fact, we should pray more fervently for the bad ones. We are not to curse them even when they're wrong. In Jude 1:8, he writes, "Likewise also these dreamers defile the flesh, reject authority, and speak evil of dignitaries." We should not curse government leaders. That doesn't mean we can't confront them, debate them, replace them in our form of government, which we have the privilege of doing. We're to respect those who have been elevated by God and hold these offices, and we're to pray for them. That doesn't mean we agree with them. Understand that loving someone enough to pray for that person does not include affirmation. I pray for political leaders with whom I have major disagreement. I do not pray that they will succeed in what they are trying to do because they are doing evil. However, I do pray that God will direct them to make the right decisions, so that our nation benefits. At the same time, it is easier to pray for those who are believers. Thankfully, we have a lot of them. Some serving in office are godly men and women, and I encourage you to pray for them.

We need to pray for our leaders. Here is why: We should be praying for them with a hope and expectation that God will lead them into an understanding of truth or at least direct their steps in their decisions so that we might live a quiet and peaceable life, able to follow and obey God ourselves. You see, we are told, whether we eat or drink, to do all for the glory of God. This is why we advocate for religious freedom so strongly. We need to be able to live out our faith. That's not just going to church; that's in the workplace. That's on the college campus. It's everywhere. We need to be able to live out our faith. Here is the clincher: It is good and acceptable in the sight of God our Savior—we are told to do this. And finally, we need to pray for leaders, as well as others, so that they may come to know Jesus Christ, for it is God's desire for all to come to know Him. That includes rulers because of the influence they have over the lives of others. We need to concern ourselves with temporal things and policies, but they must stem from a concern for the eternal. If we can zero in on the eternal—that is, man's future with God or apart from God—if we make that our priority, we get everything in between. Therefore, as often as I talk to leaders, I pray with them. Anyone I have asked to pray with or for, I've never had anyone tell me not to pray. So, I pray for them.

Finally, in 1 Timothy 2:8: "I desire therefore that the men pray everywhere, lifting up holy hands, without wrath and doubting." This is what Christians should be doing: praying to God in every place, including public spaces. It does not mean we put on a show, but we should be people of prayer. No place is off limits for us to pray. And there is something special about actually putting our feet on the ground in a particular place and praying. Then Paul talks about "lifting up holy hands," recognizing our dependence upon God and our need for Him. We do so without wrath, putting it away, forgiving others, not having bitterness in our hearts, or doubting. This goes back to the "disputing" that Paul was discussing in chapter 1, so here he encourages us instead to seek unity based on the revealed truth of God's Word.

Prayer

Father, thank You for Your word and the very clear instruction here for us to be praying for the government. We pray for those in Congress, those in state legislatures, those for governors, city councils, school board members. We especially pray, Lord, for believers You have raised up in this hour to serve in government. We pray for strength for them. We pray for encouragement for them. We pray for wisdom and insight and understanding. We pray for creative ideas for those who do not know You, Lord, who hold offices in this country. We pray for them to make the right decisions that the Holy Spirit will lead them, that You will direct them even if they are resistant to it. That it might be well for the rest of us. But we pray most of all for them, that they will come to know the truth that is found only in Jesus Christ, that they might have freedom. As Paul prayed in chapter 1, so we pray: Now to King Jesus, eternal, immortal, invisible, to God who alone is wise, be honor and glory forever and ever. Amen.

Questions for Reflection and Discussion

1. How did Paul compare himself with other sinners (see 1:15)?
    a. More righteous than some
    b. Worse than most sinners
    c. Worst sinner of all
    d. None of the above

2. Who should top our prayer list and to what end (see 2:1–4)?

Notes on Today's Bible Reading

— Day 3 —

Today's Reading: 1 Timothy 3–4

Verse of the Day

> Let no one despise your youth, but be an example to the believers in word, in conduct, in love, in spirit, in faith, in purity.
>
> — *1 Timothy 4:12*

Please read the entire Scripture selection in your own Bible and highlight or underline verses that stand out to you before you read the observations and engage the questions below.

Today we will look at two great chapters on leadership in 1 Timothy 3–4. Our key verse is 4:12: "Let no one despise your youth, but be an example to the believers in word, in conduct, in love, in spirit, in faith, in purity." In these two chapters, Paul outlines for Timothy the direction of the local church's governance. We will look at the two forms of government to which our text refers. The structure is not the most important aspect, as we will see it is the character and the conduct of the individuals in government. Quite frankly, these principles apply beyond the government of the church.

With that in mind, look at 1 Timothy 3:1–3: "This is a faithful saying: If a man desires the position of a bishop, he desires a good work. A bishop then must be blameless, the husband of one wife, temperate, sober-minded, of good behavior, hospitable, able to teach, not given to wine, not violent, not greedy for money, but gentle, not quarrelsome, not covetous." The Greek word translated "bishop" is the word from which we get "Episcopal." It refers to a person who has been given authority or responsibility to govern, and it is properly translated as "overseer." Notice how many of these qualifications deal with character and how few speak to competence. In fact, the only area of skill mentioned in these first three verses is that a leader must be "able to teach." If there is one core competency for a pastor, it is the ability to teach the Word of God in such a way that those who hear can understand and apply it so that it builds faith and Christlike behavior. Yet the dominant theme in these qualifications is that a leader himself needs to be a person of unimpeachable character.

Then Paul references another key ability regarding the leader's home life in verses 4–5: "one who rules his own house well, having his children in submission with all reverence (for if a man does not know how to rule his own house, how will he take care of the church of God?)" This leadership qualification is one that is most readily seen but is most often ignored. If you cannot manage your family or your home, how can you manage the church, a state, or a nation? This is not just a good principle. The home is a training ground for leadership, and it applies to the church. It applies to civil government as well, and indeed every form of leadership. The home is the microcosm of community, and leadership is actually birthed in the home.

Look at verse 6: "not a novice, lest being puffed up with pride he fall into the same condemnation as the devil." Maturity is important because in this culture we live in today, which idolizes youth, we often thrust young people into leadership positions. Unfortunately, most are not spiritually and emotionally ready to lead. There is much to be gained by the experience of life, and we need to be mature before we step into the pressures of leadership. Now look at verse 7: "Moreover he must have a good testimony among those who are outside, lest he fall into reproach and the snare of the devil." Paul returns to this important quality of a leader's character, but in this case his concern is about reputation outside of the church. Why? Because a leader's public character is a crucial part of his ministry. Consequently, a leader must have a good name among non-Christians to prevent the faith from being discredited. Questionable behavior before unbelievers can lead to public disgrace and create an opening for the devil to possibly ruin a ministry.

Paul goes on to provide the qualifications for deacons in verses 9–13, which is a list similar to that of the qualifications for bishop or overseer. The deacons were the servants in the church responsible for ministerial care. The deacons served and did the physical ministry of the church. They were also to be able to teach, but the elders and the bishops focused more on the spiritual needs of the church. This chapter then closes with Paul instructing Timothy on how he should organize and lead the church. Look at verse 14: "These things I write to you, though I hope to come to you shortly; but if I am delayed, I write so that you may know how you ought to conduct yourself in the house of God, which is the church of the living God, the pillar and ground of the truth."

Before we move on to chapter 4, let's circle back to the role of the church leadership and church structure and how that relates to government. There are three New Testament words that basically describe the same role: *bishop*, *elder*, and *pastor*. While "bishop" and "pastor" speak more to the role of the leader, the term "elder" is more of an honorific title attached to the office. Yet from these terms, based upon Scripture, we can delineate three primary forms of government. The Episcopal is the first form, which comes from the Greek word *episkopos*, translated as "bishop" or "overseer." Examples of this are the Anglican Church or the Episcopal Church, or even the Catholic Church. In these traditions, one leader has the authority, just like in a monarchical government with a king. The Presbyterian form of government comes from the Greek word *presbuteros*, which is translated as "elder." In this form, a body of elders has leadership or oversight of a church or churches, as opposed to one person in the Episcopal form of government. We find this in the Presbyterian Church and many other churches. The third term translated as "pastor" comes from the Greek word *poimain*. Baptist churches are most commonly known for the third form of church government that we see today, which is the congregational form. While most Baptist churches are pastor led, they are congregationally approved. The body is where the final authority rests, not with a bishop or a board of elders or even the pastor, but with the entire congregation. The congregation typically has the final say on most matters. This is the closest to a pure democracy of the forms of church government.

However, the "elder" form is closer to our republican form of government as a nation. Often, America's form of government is referred to as a democracy, but it is not a pure democracy. It is a republic. That means we get to elect leaders who then lead, and that is what an "elder" form of government is. The form of our government is important, but that is actually not the focus of this letter to Timothy. The focus is on the character and the qualifications of the leaders. No form of government can function effectively if its leaders are unqualified or of poor character. Again, these principles are true not only for the church and church government but civil government as well.

Next, let us consider verses in chapter 4: "Now the Spirit expressly says that in latter times some will depart from the faith, giving heed to deceiving spirits and doctrines of demons, speaking lies in hypocrisy, having their own conscience seared with a hot iron, forbidding to marry, and commanding to abstain from foods which God created to be received with thanksgiving by those who believe and know the truth" (vv. 1–3). This is why godly, tested, and proven leadership grounded in the Word of God is critical for the church. Now verse 4: "For every creature of God is good, and nothing is to be refused if it is received with thanksgiving; for it is sanctified by the word of God and prayer." Just a personal note from someone who lives in Louisiana. This means the fried catfish and crawfish étouffée my wife makes, while not heart-healthy, is sanctified. Because we pray over it, we can enjoy it. But I digress . . .

Notice in verse 10: "For to this end we both labor and suffer reproach, because we trust in the living God, who is the Savior of all men, especially of those who believe." Paul is saying we labor to make the Lord known, but at the same time we suffer reproach for it. Quite frankly, should we expect anything less today? Moving on to verses 11–12: "These things command and teach. Let no one despise your youth, but be an example to believers in word, in conduct, in love in spirit, in faith, in purity." Apparently in Ephesus, some were older and perhaps skeptical of young Timothy and his authority as the overseer. Consequently, Paul is saying, essentially, "Don't let these people push you around. Yet at the same time, do not give them any grounds for doing so. Lead by example." Paul reminds him (and us) that credibility in ministry does not come from age or position alone but from character. The way Timothy lived would speak louder than his age. This is where good government begins, with godly character that leads by example. Recall that Paul challenged his readers repeatedly to follow his example. This is a word to leaders, and not just those in church positions. That includes parents and grandparents. We need to lead by example in word and in godly conduct. Christian love. Filled with the Holy Spirit. Bold in the faith and purity of heart. That is a tall order. How can this possibly be done?

Well, look at verse 13: "Till I come, give attention to reading, to exhortation, to doctrine." When Paul says, "give attention to reading," that is the Word of God; and "to exhortation," that is teaching and encouraging others; and "to doctrine," that is the right application of the Word. Well, it is one thing to have the Word, but how do we apply it? That is one of the things I often pray for after our daily readings: that the Holy Spirit leads us into the application of God's Word to our lives and to the world around us. That is the doctrine. That is the application of the Word.

Then Paul urges this young leader in verse 14: "Do not neglect the gift that is in you, which was given to you by prophecy with the laying on of hands of the eldership." Again, this is not only a word to Timothy about not neglecting the God-given gift he had, but it is also a word to all of us. We all have spiritual gifts, and we need to steward those gifts well. Then in verses 15–16: "Meditate on these things; give yourself entirely to them, that your progress may be evident to all. Take heed to yourself and to the doctrine. Continue in them, for in doing this you will save both yourself and those who hear you." This concluding word to Timothy is basically "practice what you preach," and this is good advice for all leaders. These leadership qualifications may have been originally intended for church leaders, but the principles apply everywhere in the home, in business, in civil government, and in self-government. That is where it all begins. We can all benefit from Paul's leadership advice to Timothy.

Prayer

Father, thank You for Your word, and Lord, we do pray that just as Paul was instructing Timothy, that Your Holy Spirit will inspire us to know the Word, to be in the Word, but then to know how to rightfully interpret it. Lord, may our eyes be open to the truth of Your Word. May the Holy Spirit lead us in applying it to our lives. We thank You, Lord, for Your Word, and Lord, may we hide it in our hearts, and may we proclaim it with our lips that others might know. We pray in Jesus's name. Amen.

Questions for Reflection and Discussion

1. What does Paul mean when he says that both overseers/pastors and deacons should manage their families well (see 3:5, 12)?
   a. Provide spiritual leadership
   b. Provide oversight and direction
   c. Provide discipline and correction
   d. All of the above

2. What did Paul tell Timothy about those who looked down on him because of his youth and how he should live in response (see 4:12)?

Notes on Today's Bible Reading

— Day 4 —

Today's Reading: 1 Timothy 5–6

Verse of the Day

> Now godliness with contentment is great gain.
>
> — *1 Timothy 6:6*

Please read the entire Scripture selection in your own Bible and highlight or underline verses that stand out to you before you read the observations and engage the questions below.

Today we conclude our first of Paul's letters to young leaders as we look at chapters 5 and 6 of 1 Timothy. Our key verse is 1 Timothy 6:6: "Now godliness with contentment is great gain." In these final two chapters, Paul continues his practical guidance to Timothy, who had oversight of the churches in Ephesus, talking about relationships, about resources, and about responsibilities. The government in our country has grown significantly over the past century, and our national debt has expanded substantially. To put this into perspective, after the War of Independence, our new nation had a debt of $80 million. It took them thirty years to pay that debt off. Then came the Civil War, and in the aftermath, it left this nation with a debt of $2 billion. Then at the turn of the twenty-first century, we had a debt of $1 trillion. Now, a little more than two decades later, our debt stands at more than $37 trillion and counting.[2] Of course, wars and conflict have certainly contributed to our national debt, but the lion's share of our nation's annual spending, two-thirds of our budget, comes from social programs. In many ways, the church and the family have either surrendered their responsibilities, or they have been crowded out by the government, and it has come at a very high cost. With that in mind, let's look at what Paul has to say in these two chapters about relationships, about resources, and about responsibilities.

First, Paul addresses relationships beginning with 1 Timothy 5:1–3, "Do not rebuke an older man, but exhort him as a father, younger men as brothers, older women as mothers, younger women as sisters, with all purity. Honor widows who are really widows." There is a fundamental principle at work here: Treat others with honor. He begins with our elders but then includes our peers. This really gets back to the Golden Rule of Jesus, which is to treat others as we want to be treated (see Matt. 7:12).

Then note in verse 4 on the subject of widows in the church: "But if any widow has children or grandchildren, let them first show piety at home and to repay their parents; for this is good and acceptable before God." That is truly honoring parents and grandparents. In other words, we should take care of our parents and our grandparents when they are elderly and unable to take care of themselves. Next let us look further into what Paul says about widows in verses 5 and 8: "Now she who is really a widow, and left alone, trusts in God and continues in supplications and prayers night and day. . . . But if anyone does not provide for his own, and especially for those of his own household, he has denied the faith and is worse than an unbeliever." As believers, we should be taking care of our families. By God's design, the family was the first line of provision and care. Obviously, that goes beyond money. Beyond material support, it also involves purpose and mission—part of the breakdown of the transference of values from one generation to the next. What happened to that generation? Well, part of it is the physical and the emotional distance between the generations. Think about it. Grandparents have much to offer their grandchildren. They have the time and the wisdom to listen, and they just have a different perspective. They have a longer frame of reference. And that experiential wisdom can be imparted to the grandchildren. And they are the connection point from generation to generation. For a host of reasons, extended families provide a much better "daycare system" than the government.

Let's continue with what Paul has to say on this topic of widows in the church. Skip down to 1 Timothy 5:16: "If any believing man or woman has widows, let them relieve them, and do not let the church be burdened, that it may relieve those who are really widows." The church should be a safety net when the family is absent or fails. I have been a part of churches that provide for widows, and this can be done in various ways. I have been in churches where once a month they did maintenance and repair work on the cars of widows, or teams went out to do yard work and other chores for widows, or they helped them monetarily if that was needed. However, this is the role and ministry of the family first and the church second, not just the default job of the state.

Paul shifts to the responsibility of the church to meet the need of the ministers in verse 17: "Let the elders who rule well be counted worthy of double honor, especially those who labor in the word and doctrine." He is speaking of the application of that word to our lives. He continues in verse 18: "For the Scripture says, 'You shall not muzzle an ox while it treads out the grain,' and 'The laborer is worthy of his wages.'" There is nothing wrong with paying your pastor a living wage. In fact, it is essential that you do that.

Your church should be paying your pastor so that he can care for his family and focus his time and energy on leading the church to accomplish God's mission.

Next he addresses how to handle disciplinary matters involving ministers, beginning with a caution in verse 19: "Do not receive an accusation against an elder except from two or three witnesses." Now, do not miss this. The environment of the early church was similar to what we have today in this "cancel culture" and the desire to silence and discredit the church. Too many Christians today believe what they hear from the legacy media when allegations are made against spiritual leaders or other Christians in general. Unfortunately, I know that sometimes they are true, but oftentimes they are not. These allegations are designed to fracture the unity of believers, and we must be discerning in what we receive and what we believe. In verse 20, Paul instructs Timothy how to handle an elder who is guilty: "Those who are sinning rebuke in the presence of all, that the rest also may fear." Public leaders must be held accountable publicly in order to provide an example for all. Yet church discipline, done according to the Scriptures, has been lost in most churches. As a result, the church and the culture have both suffered. Then Paul gives Timothy some practical, personal advice in 5:23: "No longer drink only water, but use a little wine for your stomach's sake and your frequent infirmities." Apparently, Timothy had a weak stomach, exacerbated by all the wrangling he had to do with church members who did not respect him. Paul's prescription was more about wine having medicinal properties than it was about using it as a sedative to escape the stress of ministry.

Let's move on to chapter 6, where Paul begins by applying this principle of treating one another with honor to servants and masters, since they are both believers and brothers in the Lord (vv. 1–2).

Then Paul returns to Timothy's responsibility as a leader to ensure sound doctrine: "If anyone teaches otherwise and does not consent to wholesome words, even the words of our Lord Jesus Christ, and to the doctrine which accords with godliness, he is proud, knowing nothing, but is obsessed with disputes and arguments over words, from which come envy, strife, reviling, evil, suspicions, useless wranglings of men of corrupt minds, and destitute of the truth, who suppose that godliness is a means of gain. From such withdrawal yourself" (vv. 3–5).

Having addressed various relationships, next Paul returns to the issue of resources. What he basically says here may not be an issue of not having enough money, but the issue may not be having the right perspective on money: "Now godliness with contentment is great gain. For we brought nothing into this world, and it is certain we can carry nothing out. And having food and clothing with these we shall be content. But those who desire to be rich fall into temptation and a snare, and into many foolish and harmful lusts which drown men in destruction and perdition. For the love of money is a root of all kinds of evil, for which some have strayed from the faith in their greediness, and pierced themselves through with many sorrows" (vv. 6–10).

There is a popular misconception about money in our culture concerning what the Bible says about it. The Bible does not say, "The love of money is *the root of all evil.*" Paul plainly says in verse 10 that money is "a root of all kinds of evil." Chasing money takes us away from following Jesus and leads us down the path to sorrow and destruction. Instead, we should pursue "godliness with contentment," which will provide lasting treasure.

In fact, Paul advises Timothy to focus on this third area of responsibilities, "But you, O man of God, flee these things and pursue righteousness, godliness, faith, love, patience, gentleness. Fight the good fight of faith, lay hold on eternal life, to which you were also called and have confessed the good confession in the presence of many witnesses" (vv. 11–12). What Paul lays out here to this young leader appears to be radical concepts in the eyes of the world. However, it's only because, as a society and a nation, we have departed from the biblical principles that this nation was founded upon and guided by, up to the twentieth century. But you know what? We do not have to wait for the government to be reformed; as individuals, as families, and as churches, we can take up the responsibility that God has given to us and instructed us to assume here in the Word.

In fact, his final words in the last two verses return to this fundamental message of the Word: "O Timothy! Guard what was committed to your trust, avoiding the profane and idle babblings and contradictions of what is falsely called knowledge—by professing it some have strayed concerning the faith. Grace be with you. Amen" (vv. 20–21). The focus on the Word of God and its application to our lives as followers of Jesus cannot be overemphasized. That is central to following the Lord Jesus Christ.

Prayer

Father, we thank You for Your Word and, Lord, how it provides instruction to us in every aspect of our lives. And I know, Lord, that is criticized today. We have seen that being mocked recently in the media. But Father, I pray that will not cause us to shrink back from it, but rather it will cause us to listen in, knowing that enemies are attacking it because they know it's true. Therefore, we should cling to the Word of God. We should stand upon the Word of God. We should proclaim that Word and hold fast to the doctrine of Scripture, of the application of Your Word to our lives into the world in which we live. Give us the wisdom to do that. Give us discernment in what we believe and what we hear from the world around us. May we not believe a lie, but may we hold fast to the truth. We pray in Jesus's name. Amen.

Questions for Reflection and Discussion

1. What is Paul's opinion of a man who does not provide for his relatives and especially the members of his own immediate family (see 5:8)?
2. What does Paul describe as a root of all kinds of evil (see 6:10)?
   a. Money
   b. Love of money
   c. Both of the above
   d. Neither of the above

Notes on Today's Bible Reading

Crete

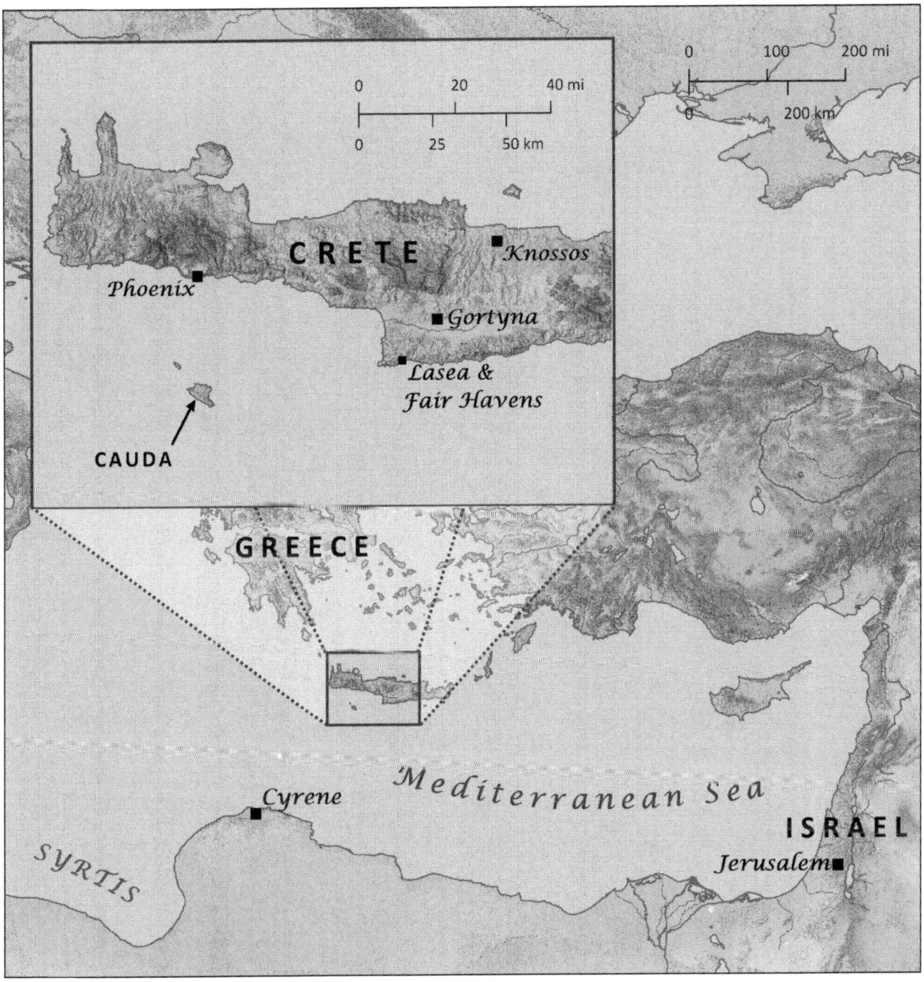
0
20
40 mi
0
25
50 km
CRETE
Knossos
Phoenix
Gortyna
Lasea &
Fair Havens
CAUDA
0
100
200 mi
0
200 km
GREECE
Mediterranean Sea
Cyrene
SYRTIS
ISRAEL
Jerusalem

— Day 5 —

Today's Reading: Titus 1–3

Verse of the Day

> Speak these things, exhort, and rebuke with all authority. Let no one despise you.
>
> — *Titus 2:15*

Please read the entire Scripture selection in your own Bible and highlight or underline verses that stand out to you before you read the observations and engage the questions below.

Today we study Paul's letter to a young leader named Titus. This is the second of Paul's pastoral letters to one of his spiritual sons. Our key verse is Titus 2:15: "Speak these things, exhort, and rebuke with all authority. Let no one despise you."

Background

Remember Paul wrote this letter sometime after his release from house arrest in Rome, after AD 62. Again, he is writing a series of letters to two of his sons in the faith, Timothy and Titus. Recall that while Timothy had a Jewish mother, Titus was a Gentile. We read about Titus in a few places in Scripture. References appear in Galatians, 2 Corinthians, and in Paul's final letter to Timothy.

Titus carried Paul's second letter to Corinth, being sent to them by Paul to help get the church in order since they had such problems. Consequently, Paul trusted Titus with oversight and leadership of the local churches. In other words, Titus must have been a wise, capable, and a spiritually discerning young leader.

Overview

This brief letter to Titus contains similar themes that we see in some of Paul's other letters. Titus was in Crete as the overseer when he received this letter. His assignment in Crete was a challenge based upon what we know about the character of the Cretans. They were known for their deception and their rebellious nature, so much so that they inspired a Greek phrase: "to cretinize"—to lie, to be deceptive. So Paul then gives Titus direction on how he should shepherd this challenging group of people. The three chapters lend themselves generally to three areas of focus. The first chapter focuses on the organization of the church, the second chapter focuses on the oracle of the church, and the third chapter focuses on the obedience of the church.

Commentary

In chapter 1, Paul lays out the need for the church to be organized and also outlines the qualifications for those who lead. These are similar to the instructions Paul sent to Timothy. Notice first of all in verse 5: "For this reason I left you in Crete, that you should set in order the things that are lacking, and appoint elders in every city as I commanded you." It should be evident by now just how much leadership is needed. Think about what happens when leadership is lacking. Division and deception, discouragement and disappointment often fill the vacuum created by the absence of godly leadership that is proficient and prepared. Leadership brings order in the midst of chaos. That is true whether it is congregational, familial, civil, or organizational.

Let's continue in Titus 1:6 for the qualifications of leaders: "if a man is blameless, the husband of one wife, having faithful children not accused of dissipation or insubordination." We see the same thing he told Timothy, that the home is the testing ground, the proving ground for leadership. Look at verses 7–8 for more qualifications: "For a bishop must be blameless, as a steward of God, not self-willed, not quick-tempered, not given to wine, not violent, not greedy for money, but hospitable, a lover of what is good, sober-minded, just, holy, self-controlled." Again, these qualities reflect the character of a godly leader as a "steward of God." But there is more that is required. Look at verse 9. "holding fast the faithful word as he has been taught, that he may be able, by sound doctrine, both to exhort and convict those who contradict." When it appears that the world is changing, and what is good is now bad and what is bad is now good (see Isa. 5:20), a godly leader holds fast to the transcendent truth of God's Word, whether it is celebrated or condemned. Yet it is not enough simply to hold onto truth personally because Paul urges Titus to share that truth, to speak God's truth to "exhort and convict" others.

Next Paul talks about the urgent need for God's truth in Titus 1:10–11: "For there are many insubordinate, both idle talkers and deceivers, especially those of the circumcision, whose mouths must be stopped, who subvert whole households, teaching things which they ought not, for the sake of dishonest gain." Notice Paul speaks of those "who subvert whole households." Remember that the churches were meeting in people's homes. Consequently, he is not only talking about deceiving a nuclear family but also a spiritual family, a whole house church. The antidote for deception is teaching the truth of God's Word.

Look at verses 12–14: "One of them, a prophet of their own, said, 'Cretans are always liars, evil beasts, lazy gluttons.' This testimony is true. Therefore rebuke them sharply, that they may be sound in the faith, not giving heed to Jewish fables and commandments of men who turn from the truth." The people in Crete had a bad reputation. In fact, the Greek word *kretidzo*, meaning "to be a Cretan," had entered the urban dictionary as slang for being an epic liar. Centuries before Paul wrote, one of their poets, Epimenides, said of Zeus and of Crete: "They fashioned a tomb for you, holy and high one, Cretans, always liars, evil beasts, idle bellies. But you are not dead: you live and abide forever, For in you we live and move and have our being."[3] That last part Paul quotes on Mars Hill in Acts 17:28, takes what is said of Zeus, and applies it to the one true God. Yet Paul picks up this derogatory quote about the Cretans and drops it into Titus 1:12. Over against the Cretan's reputation as legendary liars, Paul declares straightforwardly to Titus that God "cannot lie" (1:2).

Unfortunately, the corrupt culture of Crete had crept into the churches, and Paul directed Titus to tackle it. There are times when sharp rebukes are necessary to confront and stop those who are leading people astray. But how is that to be done from a biblical perspective? Paul turns to the oracles of the church, the Word of God. Look at Titus 2:1, "But as for you, speak the things which are proper for sound doctrine." The preaching and the teaching of the Word leads to a growing and fruitful discipleship, so churches need to be in the Word. They need to be preaching the Word. That is where we need to focus—not only on the Bible stories, which are great examples, but on biblical truths and doctrine. The doctrine is applying the Word of God to our lives.

Let's continue in Titus 2:2–5: "that the older men be sober, reverent, temperate, sound in faith, in love, in patience; the older women likewise, that they be reverent in behavior, not slanderers, not given to much wine, teachers of good things—that they admonish the young women to love their husbands, to love their children, *to be* discreet, chaste, homemakers, good, obedient to their own husbands, that the word of God may not be blasphemed." Women, mothers who have raised their children, have a tremendous role as mentors, walking alongside younger mothers who are in that period of life where it is hard to see daylight at the end of that tunnel. Those wise women can encourage them to continue on in being godly mothers and wives. The more seasoned men should be doing the same thing. Look at verse 6: "Likewise, exhort the young men to be sober-minded." Older men should help young men to realize there is more to come, and that the seeds we sow today, as young men, we reap in our later years. Therefore, we should sow good seed.

Next consider verses 7–10: "in all things showing yourself *to be* a pattern of good works; in doctrine *showing* integrity, reverence, incorruptibility, sound speech that cannot be condemned, that one who is an opponent may be ashamed, having nothing evil to say of you. Exhort bondservants to be obedient to their own masters, to be well pleasing in all things, not answering back, not pilfering, but showing all good fidelity, that they may adorn the doctrine of God our Savior in all things." This is talking about the workplace. We need to be faithful to work hard for our employers, doing a good job, pursuing excellence. Why? Because our work ethic and attitude has a direct reflection on our Savior.

Finishing in Titus 2: "For the grace of God that brings salvation has appeared to all men, teaching us that, denying ungodliness and worldly lusts, we should live soberly, righteously, and godly in the present age, looking for the blessed hope and glorious appearing of our great God and Savior Jesus Christ, who gave Himself for us, that He might redeem us from every lawless deed and purify for Himself His own special people, zealous for good works. Speak these things, exhort, and rebuke with all authority. Let no one despise you" (vv. 11–15). Paul is instructing Timothy to help these young men and women to have an eternal perspective, knowing that they are looking for that blessed hope, that glorious appearing of their great God and Savior. We've got to look beyond the temporal and the pleasures of this life to the eternal. Our hope for the future should shape how we live today.

Then in chapter 3, we have the next section I am referring to as the obedience of the church. Look where that obedience begins in verses 1–2: "Remind them to be subject to rulers and authorities, to obey, to be ready for every good work, to speak evil of no one, to be peaceable, gentle, showing all humility to all men." Some might say, "Wait a minute, how does that line up with what Peter and John said to those religious rulers when they said we should obey God rather than men?" (See Acts 5:20.) Quite frankly, it lines up perfectly. Our attitude and disposition should be one of submission to the authorities God has established. Whether it be to civil government or the church, whatever form of government, our attitude should be one of submission and obedience. Disobedience is a last resort when earthly authorities command a believer to do something that contradicts the Word of God.

What Paul is writing about here is really a heart issue—it is about attitude. We should not be looking for the next faith-based fight or conflict. We should seek to live in peace, being gentle, showing humility to all men. However, that does not mean that we compromise the truth. We do not seek peace at any price; we do not avoid conflict if it means sacrificing truth. There is a red line for every believer, and it is the Word of God. Remember the purpose of our lives as followers of Jesus is to bring glory to God in how we conduct ourselves in every situation. This is especially important for us today in a culture where our civil government is becoming more hostile toward biblical Christianity. We should not be looking for conflict, but we should not run from conflict either.

Let's continue in Titus 3:

> For we ourselves were also once foolish, disobedient, deceived, serving various lusts and pleasures, living in malice and envy, hateful and hating one another. But when the kindness and the love of God our Savior toward man appeared, not by works of righteousness which we have done, but according to His mercy He saved us, through the washing of regeneration and renewing of the Holy Spirit, whom He poured out on us abundantly through Jesus Christ our Savior, that having been justified by His grace we should become heirs according to the hope of eternal life. This is a faithful saying, and these things I want you to affirm constantly, that those who have believed in God should be careful to maintain good works. These things are good and profitable to men. (vv. 3–8)

It is not just enough to make a profession of faith; we must live out that faith. That is why we advocate for religious freedom. Allow me to explain. The religious freedom I have spent most of my time at the Family Research Council advocating for is our ability to live out our faith in every aspect of our lives. Those are the good works Paul is talking about here. As he says, these things are good and profitable to men—not just us but to everyone.

Consider this final section, beginning with verse 9: "But avoid foolish disputes, genealogies, contentions, and strivings about the law; for they are unprofitable and useless." Focus on what is important. Paul continues in verses 10–11: "Reject a divisive man after the first and second admonition, knowing that such a person is warped and sinning, being self-condemned." Again, the Cretans were unruly and rebellious. As believers, our default position in Christ Jesus should be to obey authorities. However, that does not mean there aren't times when we must take a stand against unrighteous edicts. Resistance should not be our default position—obedience should be.

This is another remarkable letter filled with much insight—and not just to the church Titus was leading but to the entire church. Therefore, I encourage you to meditate upon this Word and pray about how the Lord might use it in your life to strengthen you in your walk with Him so that others will see your good works and men will be blessed by your obedience to God.

Prayer

Father, we thank You for Your Word. Lord, I pray that the Holy Spirit will speak to our hearts and show us how we might apply this to our lives today. So, Lord, that through our good works, through our obedience to You, living out our faith in Jesus Christ, that it will be done in such a way that all men will be blessed, that the world around us will be a better place because of our faithfulness to You. We pray this in Jesus's name, Amen.

Questions for Reflection and Discussion

1. What were the older women to teach the younger women (see 2:4–5)?
   a. Love their husbands and children
   b. Be self-controlled, pure, working at home, kind
   c. Submissive to their own husbands
   d. All of the above

2. What is the basis of our salvation (see 3:4–5)?

Notes on Today's Bible Reading

Paul's Imprisonment

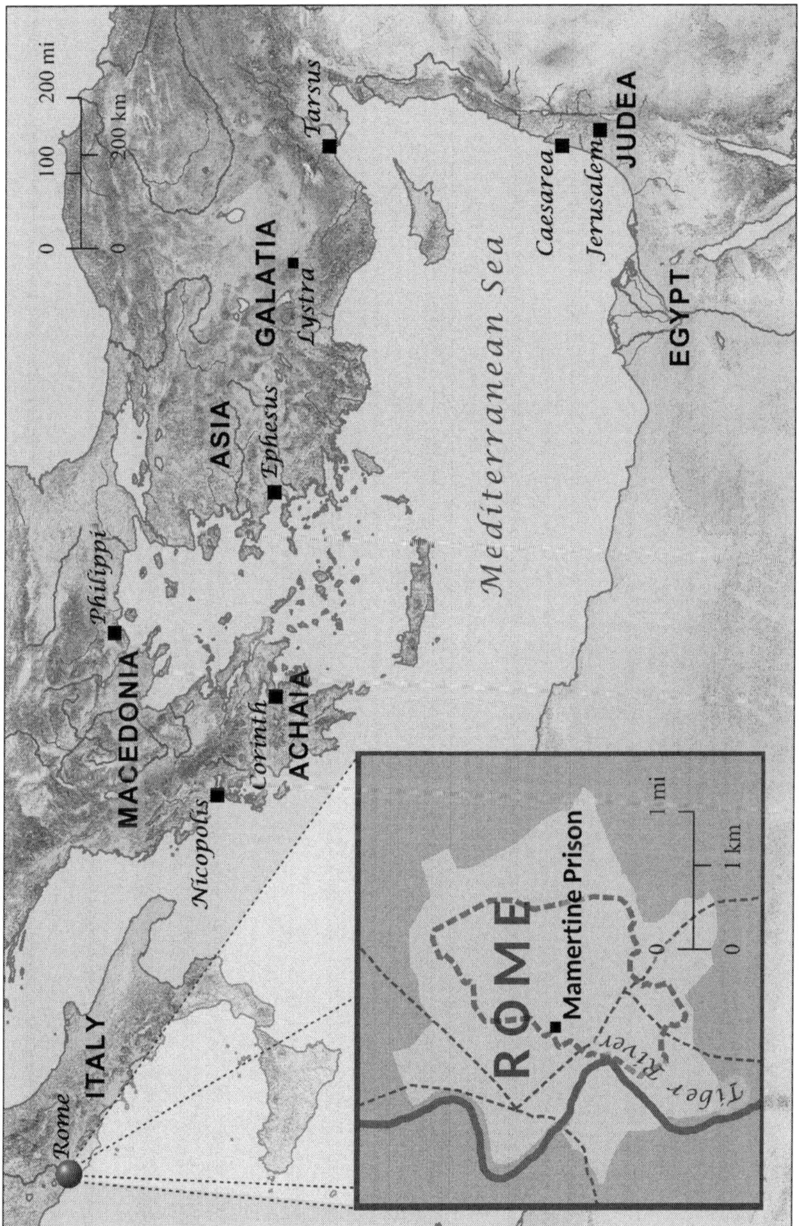

— Day 6 —

Today's Reading: 2 Timothy 1–2

Verses of the Day

> You therefore must endure hardship as a good soldier of Jesus Christ.
>
> *— 2 Timothy 2:3*

Please read the entire Scripture selection in your own Bible and highlight or underline verses that stand out to you before you read the observations and engage the questions below.

We begin the final letter that Paul wrote, and it is also addressed to Timothy. In today's study, we will consider the first two chapters. Paul wrote this letter during his final imprisonment in Rome just prior to his execution by Emperor Nero in AD 66–67. Our key verse is 2 Timothy 2:3: "You therefore must endure hardship as a good soldier of Jesus Christ."

Do you remember the old hymn "Onward Christian Soldiers"? As a boy in our small Presbyterian church, I recall singing that song. I like the song, and unfortunately, today you would have a hard time finding it in most churches. All the mainline denominations that still use hymnals have removed the song from hymnbooks. Why? Because it has been declared to be militaristic. In fact, one author suggested that the hymn was dangerous because it perpetuated the acceptability of religious warfare.[4] This is what happens when you depart from Scripture because Paul is the one who described what we are engaged in as "warfare," right?

In this letter written to his spiritual son, Timothy, Paul reminds him in verses 3–4: "You therefore must endure hardship as a good soldier of Jesus Christ. No one engaged in warfare entangles himself with the affairs of this life, that he may please him who enlisted him as a soldier." When you are engaged in warfare, it is a matter of life and death. Therefore, you are really focused because not only does your life depend on it, but the lives of others are at stake, and your mission is at risk. Paul is equating what we have been called to do in the kingdom of God with the battle of a good soldier. This call to endure difficulty and even stand alone in pursuit of the mission we have been given to advance the Kingdom is central to this entire letter of Paul's writing to Timothy.

As mentioned before, Paul wrote this letter during his second imprisonment, which was much different than the first, when he was in a rented house. He was chained to a Roman guard, but he had some freedom, such as the ability to entertain guests. So, it really was not all that bad. This final imprisonment, however, is much different—he is in a dungeon. Scripture does not address the cause of Paul's second arrest, but some historians suggest that he and other Christians were falsely accused by Nero of being involved in the fire that destroyed Rome in AD 64.[5] As the persecution under Emperor Nero was in full swing, shortly after this writing, church tradition says that Paul was beheaded.

Now look at 2 Timothy 1:3: "I thank God, whom I serve with a pure conscience, as my forefathers did, as without ceasing I remember you in my prayers night and day." Paul is saying: "Timothy, I am praying for you day and night." We see this repeatedly with Paul. He was a man of prayer.

He continues in verses 4–5: "greatly desiring to see you, being mindful of your tears, that I may be filled with joy, when I call to remembrance that genuine faith that is in you, which dwelt first in your grandmother Lois and your mother Eunice, and I am persuaded is in you also." What a great legacy! Timothy was blessed with a godly mother and grandmother. You know you never know the impact you will have on your children and grandchildren, but it can be a good one if you are faithful in serving God, praying for, and instilling that biblical faith into your loved ones.

Now notice in verse 6: "Therefore I remind you to stir up the gift of God which is in you through the laying on of my hands." So how was Timothy to be a good soldier? How are we to be good Christian soldiers? Paul says here, "stir up the gift of God," that is, rekindle that gift. Like a fire that is starting to go out, you stir up the ashes, and it ignites and begins to blaze again. You may recall this is similar to what Paul said in Ephesians 5:18 about being filled with the Spirit. We have a responsibility. It doesn't just happen. The Spirit does not just fall on you without spiritual preparation. We have to actively pursue the Spirit's filling, and so it is with the Spirit's enabling.

Next let's look at verse 7: "for God has not given us a spirit of fear, but of power and of love and of a sound mind. We cannot operate in fear if we are going to be a good soldier. In fact, the Greek word translated "fear" is different than what we see in almost every other case in the New Testament. Typically the word *phobos* is used, and from that Greek word, we get our word "phobia." But that is not the word used here. In verse 7 the Greek word is *deilia*, which is more accurately described as "cowardice." In fact, *deilia* is only used on two other occasions in the New Testament. One was when the disciples thought the ship was going to sink, and they woke up Jesus and he chided them (see Matt. 8:26; Mark 4:40). The second instance is in Revelation 21:8: "But the cowardly [that is the *deilos*], unbelieving, abominable, murderers, sexually immoral, sorcerers, idolaters, and all liars shall have their part in the lake which burns with fire and brimstone, which is the second death." So, Paul is not just telling Timothy, "Don't be afraid"; in reality he is saying, "Don't be cowardly."

Let's continue on with 2 Timothy 1:8: "Therefore do not be ashamed of the testimony of our Lord, nor of me His prisoner, but share with me in the sufferings for the gospel according to the power of God." This is critical. Put that verse together with what Paul writes down in verse 15: "This you know, that all those in Asia have turned away from me." Why? Because he is in chains—being in prison was not respectable. Additionally, the Roman government was after Paul. Perhaps believers were thinking, "If we hang around Paul, we could be next." Consequently, Paul tells Timothy, "Do not be ashamed of the testimony of our Lord." Indeed, Jesus Himself was rejected, labeled a glutton and a drunkard, called a blasphemer and even demon possessed. So, He was arrested, scourged, and crucified." Yet Paul pleads with Timothy not to be ashamed of suffering with the Lord, and "Timothy, don't be ashamed of 'me His prisoner, but share with me in the sufferings for the gospel.'"

Now here is the truth. If we are ashamed of those who suffer for their stand for the Lord, it is likely that we will not stand when it is our turn. We will probably compromise. We will probably say what we need to in order to sidestep public shaming, the cancel culture, or physical suffering in persecution. So, if we are ashamed of those who are being persecuted for their stand for the Lord, chances are great that we will not stand when our time comes to stand for Jesus.

Paul goes on in verses 9–12:

> [W]ho has saved us and called us with a holy calling, not according to our works, but according to His own purpose and grace which was given to us in Christ Jesus before time began, but has now been revealed by the appearing of our Savior Jesus Christ, who has abolished death and brought life and immortality to light through the gospel, to which I was appointed a preacher, an apostle, and a teacher of the Gentiles. For this reason I also suffer these things; nevertheless I am not ashamed, for I know whom I have believed and am persuaded that He is able to keep what I have committed to Him until that Day.

Now this is a revealing and challenging statement Paul wrote: "I'm in prison about to be executed because I am a follower of Jesus Christ. Yet far from being ashamed, I am confident, not in what I am seeing and not what I am experiencing right now, but in the word and the promises of God.

Continue next to verse 13: "Hold fast the pattern of sound words which you have heard from me, in faith and love which are in Christ Jesus." Once again, Paul makes clear the Word of God is central to our ability to faithfully serve the Lord. Then Paul says, "That good thing which was committed to you, keep by the Holy Spirit who dwells in us" (v. 14). If you want to be a good soldier, rekindle your love and passion for the Lord. Operate from His power with love and a sound mind. Do not be ashamed of the rebukes of this world. Embrace it. Stand firm on the Word of God regardless of what others think, say, or do.

Let's move on to chapter 2: "You therefore, my son, be strong in the grace that is in Christ Jesus" (v. 1) This reminds me of what Paul wrote in Ephesians 6:10: "[B]e strong in the Lord and in the power of His might." We are to be strong in the Lord and in His grace. Next Paul brings up the importance of making disciples in 2 Timothy 2:2: "And the things that you have heard from me among many witnesses, commit these to faithful men who will be able to teach others also." In other words, invest your life in others who will continue this process of teaching and discipling, which is the fulfillment of the Great Commission of Christ (see Matt. 28:18–20). Paul continues in 2 Timothy 2:3–4: "You therefore must endure hardship as a good soldier of Jesus Christ. No one engaged in warfare entangles himself with the affairs of this life, that he may please him who enlisted him as a soldier." He is talking about the sacrifices we will make and the difficulties we will encounter as followers of Jesus. It is like being in the military. It takes living a disciplined and unencumbered life so that we can respond to our call to duty with effectiveness and excellence.

Look down at verses 8–9: "Remember that Jesus Christ, of the seed of David, was raised from the dead according to my gospel, for which I suffer trouble as an evildoer, even to the point of chains; but the word of God is not chained." Don't miss what Paul is saying here: "I preached this gospel, and as a result I am in chains but not the Word of God. The Word of God cannot be chained. It goes forth with power and with great effect!" Then Paul apparently quotes an early Christian hymn or creed in verses, which he labels as a "faithful saying" (vv. 11–13):

For if we died with Him,
We shall also live with Him.
If we endure,
We shall also reign with Him.
If we deny Him,
He also will deny us.
If we are faithless,
He remains faithful;
He cannot deny Himself.

We often want the glory, but we do not want the suffering. Yet if we want the glory that comes with being associated with Jesus Christ, we must go through the suffering. We must endure the rejection.

Paul goes on to issue some cautions against getting off track, and the solution is to stick with the Word of God. Notice in verses 14–16: "Remind them of these things, charging them before the Lord not to strive about words to no profit, to the ruin of the hearers. Be diligent to present yourself approved to God, a worker who does not need to be ashamed, rightly dividing the word of truth. But shun profane and idle babblings, for they will increase to more ungodliness." In other words, stay focused; do not go off on tangents. Then Paul expresses concern over the outcome of frivolous pursuits in verses 17–19: "And their message will spread like cancer. Hymenaeus and Philetus are of this sort, who have strayed concerning the truth, saying that the resurrection is already past; and they overthrow the faith of some. Nevertheless the solid foundation of God stands, having this seal: 'The Lord knows those who are His,' and, 'Let everyone who names the name of Christ depart from iniquity.'" If we stay on the firm foundation of God's Word, we can avoid the snares of the enemy and help others who get caught.

In this final section, Paul speaks of avoiding temptation by pursuing personal holiness. Continue in verses 20–21: "But in a great house there are not only vessels of gold and silver, but also of wood and clay, some for honor and some for dishonor. Therefore if anyone cleanses himself from the latter, he will be a vessel for honor, sanctified and useful for the Master, prepared for every good work."

Then Paul closes out with practical advice for Timothy, which we would do well to hear and apply. Look at the first portion of verse 22: "Flee also youthful lusts; but pursue righteousness." Don't miss this. Paul is saying, "Run from sexual temptation, but run after righteousness." Pursue "righteousness, faith, love, peace with those who call on the Lord out of a pure heart." But notice he comes back to the topic of fruitless arguments in verse 23: "But avoid foolish and ignorant disputes, knowing that they generate strife." Here we go again. He is drilling this into Timothy, and we should heed his words, about being a poor steward of our time by engaging in disputes over nonessential preferences and fringe issue nonsense that accomplishes nothing except division and strife. He goes on to say in verses 24–26: "And a servant of the Lord must not quarrel but be gentle to all, able to teach, patient, in humility correcting those who are in opposition, if God perhaps will grant them repentance, so that they may know the truth, and that they may come to their senses and escape the snare of the devil, having been taken captive by him to do his will." May the Lord help us as leaders take these words to heart.

Prayer

Heavenly Father, thank You for Your Word and this letter that Paul wrote to Timothy, offering such practical advice, and here at the end of his life when he knew this was the end, as we see that later in this letter. Lord, I pray that we will be strengthened and will know that our hope is in You—not what we see, not what we feel, not what we read. Help us remember what we know to be true in Your Word: You never change; You are the same yesterday, today, and forever, and we can anchor our lives to You. So I pray that You will help us once again to rightfully apply Your Word and the power of the Holy Spirit to our lives. Lord, make us into effective ambassadors for Your Kingdom, that others will see the peace and the joy that marks our lives. And we pray that we might be able to share, as Peter said, about the hope that is within us. We pray this in Jesus's name. Amen.

Questions for Reflection and Discussion

1. God has not given us a spirit of fear but of what (see 1:7)?
   a. Power
   b. Love
   c. Self-control/sound mind
   d. All of the above

2. What was Timothy to do with the teaching from Paul (see 2:2)?

Notes on Today's Bible Reading

— Day 7 —

Today's Reading: 2 Timothy 3–4

Verse of the Day

> Yes, and all who desire to live godly in Christ Jesus will suffer persecution.
>
> — *2 Timothy 3:12*

Please read the entire Scripture selection in your own Bible and highlight or underline verses that stand out to you before you read the observations and engage the questions below.

Today, we have the final recorded words of the indefatigable apostle Paul as he concludes his second letter to Timothy. As we look at chapters 3 and 4, our key verse is 3:12: "Yes, and all who desire to live godly in Christ Jesus will suffer persecution." In view of the inevitable hardship and persecution, could that be why Jesus described the path to abundant life as narrow and the gate to destruction broad? That the travelers on the narrow path are few and those on the broad path are many? Regardless, Paul is underscoring the fact that there is a cost to being a true disciple of Jesus Christ.

Let's dive into chapter 3: "But know this, that in the last days perilous [difficult or stressful] times will come: For men will be lovers of themselves, lovers of money, boasters, proud, blasphemers, disobedient to parents, unthankful, unholy, unloving, unforgiving, slanderers, without self-control, brutal, despisers of good, traitors, headstrong, haughty, lovers of pleasure rather than lovers of God, having a form of godliness but denying its power. And from such people turn away!" (vv. 1–5). Those of you who are students of the Bible, and especially Paul's letters, will notice that this list is similar to the characteristics of fallen mankind in Romans 1:29–31. However, the people Paul is describing in Romans are obviously lost. In 2 Timothy, Paul seems to be describing people in the church. He is saying the church will be filled with those whose conduct is indistinguishable from the world, except that it will be cloaked with this form of religiosity but void of the vitality of a real relationship with the Lord.

Paul continues in verses 6–7: "For of this sort are those who creep into households and make captives of gullible women loaded down with sins, led away by various lusts, always learning and never able to come to the knowledge of the truth." This is an important description because they are looking for the latest and greatest—the latest revelation, the latest "word"—and they are running here and there and everywhere but never discovering the truth that is right before them. This is true of many believers today. They are always looking for a word for revelation from God when it is right in there in the Word of God. We need to speak the Word of God. He is not going to give us more until we have consumed what He has given us already, and that is His Word.

Let's consider verses 8–9: "Now as Jannes and Jambres resisted Moses, so do these also resist the truth: men of corrupt minds, disapproved concerning the faith; but they will progress no further, for their folly will be manifest to all, as theirs also was." These were the names that Jewish tradition had assigned to the Egyptian magicians who had opposed Moses in Egypt. Paul is saying that they were exposed. They came to nothing, and so will those who are attempting to lead people astray. Next look at verses 10–11: "But you have carefully followed my doctrine, manner of life, purpose, faith, longsuffering, love, perseverance, persecutions, afflictions, which happened to me at Antioch, at Iconium, at Lystra—what persecutions I endured. And out of them all the Lord delivered me." Paul tells Timothy here, in his final correspondence, to follow his example and trust God.

It seems that since the writing of this letter, the progression of what he described here has continued, although there have been periods of reprieve. As the influence of the church grew during the past two thousand years, it had a profound effect on society. Jesus said we are salt and light, and that salt has a preserving effect. Light leads the way. However, as the church recedes, evil advances. I argue that, today, what we see in society is that the church, for the most part, has receded. It has withdrawn into the four walls of its building. As a result, we see lawlessness on the streets of our cities. For example, we have seen in Washington pro-Hamas demonstrators, tens of thousands of them yelling "Allahu Akbar" at the White House, pushing on the gates. I argue this is a symptom of a church that has been in retreat.

Note Paul's warning to Timothy in verse 12: "Yes, and all who desire to live godly in Christ Jesus will suffer persecution." Now he begins to lay out where spiritual apostasy will lead. This is not much different than the warning that Jesus gave in John 15:18–19: "If the world hates you, you know that it hated Me before it hated you. If you were of the world, the world would love its own. Yet because you are not of the world, but I chose you out of the world, therefore the world hates you." See, the world hates us because we represent God, and the more a society turns from God, it embraces a hatred of God. Then Jesus said in verse 20, "Remember the word that I said to you, 'A servant is not greater than his master.' If they persecuted Me, they will also persecute you. If they kept My word, they will keep yours also." This moral and cultural corruption that we see today stems from spiritual apostasy. Furthermore, this corruption flows from the persecution of the followers of Christ. You have apostasy, so the church loses its power and its influence. Corruption comes in. And then, from that, persecution arises in the broader society. So how do you get back? Well, it is simple: You go back to the Word of God.

Let's look at 2 Timothy 3:13: "But evil men and impostors will grow worse and worse, deceiving and being deceived." These deceivers will be so good that they deceive themselves. You know, the spiritual, moral, and cultural corruption will, apparently, according to what Paul is saying here, intensify as we move closer to the end of the age. That is what Jesus says. That is what the Word of God says. With that in mind, what are the safeguards that Paul provides for Timothy to prevent true believers from being led astray by these deceptive and false teachers? Because God has called us to be faithful regardless of the times, how do we prevent becoming discouraged as these days grow dark?

The answer is in verse 14: "continue"—the one key word. "But you must continue in the things which you have learned and been assured of, knowing from whom you have learned them" (v. 14). Paul is saying to Timothy, "Continue in what I have taught you. It does not matter if it is not popular, nor does it matter if it is rejected by the broader culture. Continue in that!" In fact, Timothy had a faithful mother and grandmother who impressed the Word of God on his heart when he was just a boy: "from childhood you have known the Holy Scriptures, which are able to make you wise for salvation through faith which is in Christ Jesus" (v. 15). Again, Paul is saying, "Continue in that!" George Barna, who is a Senior Fellow at the Family Research Council, has conducted research that indicates a worldview is shaped in childhood between fifteen months and thirteen years of age. That is when our basis for interpreting the world's events is formed. This is why the world wants to get them at earlier and earlier ages. Therefore, if we want them to have a biblical worldview, we need to be teaching our children the Scripture—not only Bible stories but biblical truths, even in these young ages.

Verse 16: "All Scripture is given by inspiration of God, and is profitable for doctrine, for reproof, for correction, for instruction in righteousness, that the man of God may be complete, thoroughly equipped for every good work." In light of what we just read, what is the answer? How do we prevent being deceived? How do we keep from being discouraged? The Word—it is Scripture. The Word makes us wise unto salvation. Paul says that by grace through faith it provides teaching on how to live. It provides reproof and correction, pointing them to God. It provides correction or discipleship through discipline. It provides instruction and training in righteousness so that the child of God will be complete or perfectly prepared for the call that God has on them. Therefore, we must be in the Word of God. That is why we are doing this journey. It's why I encourage you to invite others to join us.

Paul continues this line of exhortation into 2 Timothy 4: "I charge you therefore before God and the Lord Jesus Christ, who will judge the living and the dead at His appearing and His kingdom: Preach the word! Be ready in season and out of season. Convince, rebuke, exhort, with all longsuffering and teaching" (vv. 1–2). Proclaim the truth, he says, when it is welcomed and when it's not welcome. Proclaim the truth when it is convenient to you and proclaim the truth when it is inconvenient to you.

Next look at verse 3: "For the time will come when they will not endure sound doctrine, but according to their own desires, because they have itching ears, they will heap up for themselves teachers; and they will turn their ears away from the truth, and be turned aside to fables." There will be those in the church who will leave sound teaching to find voices that affirm their choices, which contradict Scripture. However, Paul goes on to tell Timothy how to respond in verse 5: "But you be watchful in all things, endure afflictions, do the work of an evangelist, fulfill your ministry." He is saying, do not change your message. Do not chase after those who have departed from the truth. Yes, we want to declare it to them, but we're not trying to change the message. Do not change your message to try to keep them there. Rather, endure the affliction. Endure the ridicule. Endure the rejection that may come as people walk out of your church or walk away from friendship with you—even if it means outright prosecution or persecution, as Paul experienced in that dungeon in Rome.

Finally, let's look at Paul's closing declaration in verses 7–8: "I have fought the good fight, I have finished the race, I have kept the faith. Finally, there is laid up for me the crown of righteousness, which the Lord, the righteous Judge, will give me on that Day, and not to me only, but also to all who have loved His appearing." This is powerful. Looking back over his life in Christ and all that he had been through, and all the relationships and all of the encounters and all of the persecution, Paul says, I have no regrets. I have fought the good fight. I have finished my race. I have kept the faith. So how do we live in such a way that we can make the same declaration as we follow Jesus in these perilous days in which we live?

In verse 16 Paul says, "At my first defense no one stood with me, but all forsook me. May it not be charged against them." This is interpreted differently, but many see this when he was charged during his second imprisonment in Rome; everyone abandoned him. The persecution of Christians was becoming widespread, and no one wanted to be associated with someone who was seen as a ringleader. Again, they accused him. Tradition holds that Nero accused him of being a ringleader in starting the fire that burned down Rome. No one wanted to stand around Paul, so everybody ran from him. In verse 17, "But the Lord stood with me and strengthened me, so that the message might be preached fully through me, and that all the Gentiles might hear. Also I was delivered out of the mouth of the lion. And the Lord will deliver me from every evil work and preserve me for His heavenly kingdom. To Him be glory forever and ever. Amen!"

Following the account of the early church historian Eusebius, *Foxe's Book of Martyrs* records that Paul was led by Nero's soldiers "out of the city to the place of execution, where he, after his prayers made, gave his neck to the sword."[6] Yet, like Paul, when we stand for the Lord, anchored to the Word of the Lord, even if it means we must stand alone in reality, we are not alone. Jesus will stand with us to strengthen us so that we, too, can say, I have fought the good fight. I have finished my race. I have kept the faith.

Prayer

Father, thank You for this enlightening, challenging, and encouraging word from Paul as he writes what we have as his final instructions to young Timothy. Lord, I pray that at the end of our lives, we will live in such a way that we can make the same declaration Paul did, that we have fought the good fight. We have finished our race. We have kept the faith. May the Holy Spirit guide us through Your Word, showing us how to apply Your Word to our lives and then yielding to it regardless of what the culture says. May we stand firm knowing that You stand beside us, and may we do so with joy and with peace—not with trepidation, not with anxiety, but peace and joy. We pray this in Jesus's name. Amen.

Questions for Reflection and Discussion

1. What is Scripture useful for (see 3:16)?
2. What reasons did Paul give that he was ready to meet the Lord (see 4:6–8)?
   a. He fought the good fight.
   b. He finished the race.
   c. He kept the faith.
   d. All of the above

Notes on Today's Bible Reading

Conclusion

As we conclude our study of Paul's letters to leaders, I thought it would be helpful to zoom out and consider some of the key themes as well as make some contemporary applications.

Key Themes in the Pastoral Epistles

1. **Sufficiency of the Scriptures** – Paul points to the Spirit-inspired Word of God as the authoritative and sufficient guide for faith and practice. It is God's manual for leadership and life.
2. **Sound Doctrine and the Centrality of the Gospel** – It follows that Paul warns both Timothy and Titus to guard against false teachers who pervert the clear teachings of Scripture (1 Tim. 1:3–7; Titus 1:10–16) and to hold firmly to the truth of the gospel (2 Tim. 1:13–14).
3. **Character of Leadership** – Leadership is not about possessing personal charisma or a dominant personality, but it is about demonstrating humility and integrity, faithfulness and holiness (1 Tim. 3:1–13; Titus 1:5–9).
4. **Perseverance in Ministry** – Both Timothy and Titus are urged to endure hardship, correct with patience, and remain steadfast in the mission (2 Tim. 2:1–6; Titus 2:15).

5. **Passing the Torch** – Perhaps most poignantly, Paul stresses the need for mentoring. He urged Timothy, "And the things that you have heard from me . . . commit these to faithful men who will be able to teach others also" (2 Tim. 2:2). He told Titus, "appoint elders in every city as I commanded you" (1:5). This creates a chain of discipleship that extends far beyond Paul's lifetime into the future.

Contemporary Applications

First, Paul models what it means to invest deeply in others for the sake of the gospel. His relationship with Timothy and Titus was not superficial; he poured his life, wisdom, and heart into these younger men. Today, the church desperately needs seasoned believers willing to do the same. Those who serve as mentors must:

- **Be intentional** – Paul chose Timothy deliberately (Acts 16:3) and entrusted him with significant tasks. Mature Christians should prayerfully identify emerging leaders to nurture.
- **Model Christlikeness** – Paul said, "Imitate me, just as I also imitate Christ" (1 Cor. 11:1). Mentors must live out what they teach.
- **Provide encouragement and correction** – Paul both affirmed Timothy's sincere faith (2 Tim. 1:5) and challenged him to boldness (2 Tim. 1:7–8). Mentorship requires both affirmation and accountability.
- **Prepare for succession** – Paul knew his race was nearly finished (2 Tim. 4:6–7), but he was confident the gospel would continue through Timothy, Titus, and others. Mature believers must think generationally, ensuring that leadership is multiplied.

Second, young leaders like Timothy and Titus exemplify what it looks like to be teachable and faithful apprentices. They were willing to serve alongside Paul, often in difficult contexts, and to receive both encouragement and correction. For aspiring leaders today, their example offers practical guidance:

- **Be teachable** – Timothy's humility and openness to Paul's instruction allowed him to grow in wisdom and leadership. Aspiring leaders must be willing to submit to authority, listen, learn, pivot, and adjust.
- **Cultivate faithfulness** – Both Timothy and Titus demonstrated reliability, which earned Paul's trust. Faithful service in small things often leads to greater responsibilities.
- **Endure hardship** – Paul warned Timothy that ministry would involve suffering (2 Tim. 3:12). Young leaders today must be prepared to endure challenges from a hostile culture with courage and perseverance.
- **Prioritize character over competence** – Paul emphasized godly living above all else. Skills are important, but integrity and holiness are essential for lasting influence. Competence can be gained with experience and effort, but there is no substitute for character.
- **Sufficiency of God's Word** – Paul always directed these leaders back to the Scriptures as the manual for leadership and kingdom living. As he put it to Timothy: "All Scripture is given by inspiration of God, and is profitable for doctrine, for reproof, for correction, for instruction in righteousness, that the man of God may be complete, thoroughly equipped for every good work" (2 Tim. 3:16–17). He also encouraged Titus: "holding fast the faithful word as he has been taught,

that he may be able, by sound doctrine, both to exhort and convict those who contradict" (1:9). The Scriptures are the sufficient and faithful foundation for leaders, and indeed all followers of Christ.

The Ongoing Call of Raising Young Leaders

The Pastoral Epistles remind us that the mission of the church is bigger than any single leader. Paul knew his time was short, but he entrusted the gospel to the next generation. That chain of discipleship has reached us, and now we bear responsibility for carrying it forward. For mentors, the call is clear: Identify, invest in, and empower younger leaders. For younger leaders, the challenge is equally pressing: Be faithful, teachable, and courageous. The health of the church depends on this ongoing partnership between generations. In a world where leadership is often measured by charisma, influence, or popularity, the Pastoral Epistles call us back to biblical essentials: sound doctrine, godly character, persevering faith, and intentional mentoring. The legacies of Paul and of his young protégés, Timothy and Titus, continue to inspire us. The question remains, Who will step up today—whether as a Paul passing the torch, a Timothy, or a Titus receiving it—to ensure that the gospel is faithfully proclaimed to the next generation?

Appendix 1:
Stand on the Word Bible Reading Plan

Visit frc.org/Bible for our chronological journey through the Bible that we call "Stand on the Word." We encourage you to spend time reading and studying the Bible because it is literally "God-breathed" (2 Tim. 3:16 NIV); it is God's very words to us. The Bible answers the big questions, such as, Why am I here? Where did I come from? Where am I going (life after death)? If God is good, why does evil and suffering exist? The Bible not only answers these big questions; it offers practical advice in areas such as, How can I deal with feelings of fear or anger or guilt? How can I forgive when I cannot forget? What should I look for in a spouse? How can I have a successful marriage? How can I be a good parent? What is my spiritual gift and place in the church? What is my stewardship responsibility as a citizen? We learned the verse in Bible school, "Your word is a lamp to my feet and a light to my path" (Ps. 119:105). God's Word shows us the way forward in any area of life and on every question we face.

The Stand on the Word Bible Reading Plan takes us through the Bible chronologically. In other words, each reading takes us through the Bible as events occurred in history as far as it is possible. Here is how it works for our family. At the same time each morning, whether I am at home, in Washington, or some foreign country, I send my wife and children a morning greeting along with a reminder of the passage for the day. The text includes two questions related to the reading. The questions are designed to help in content retention, serve as an accountability tool, and provide for discussion.

The two-year plan does not have a Sunday passage. Instead, it provides an outline for a family discussion that can be done on Sunday afternoon or evening. Our family has incorporated the discussion into our Sunday lunch, which follows a biblical model of life enriching conversations over a meal. The weekly discussion time begins with a spiritual leader asking each person individually for one or two insights or truths they gained from their reading during the week and how those truths apply to our lives. After everyone else shares, the father or group leader can lead a short discussion of one of the passages that was read during the week and how it applies to our lives here and now. It is also a time for them to ask questions.

By the way, you don't have to have all the answers. If you don't know, tell them so, then talk to your pastor or other trusted person with Bible knowledge. If your children start asking questions, that suggests they are thinking about what they are reading.

Reading God's Word will help you establish a fruitful walk with the God who made you and loves you. Whether you are single or married, this plan will enable you to lead your friends and family in daily reading God's Word. The added benefit is that you will all be reading the same text together. It will amaze you to see how God speaks sometimes in the same ways and at other times in different ways to each of you. Being on this journey together will build a spiritual synergy, a deep bond, and sense of unity and purpose like nothing else! Use it to impart the Word of life. Visit frc.org/Bible to sign up or simply download the Stand Firm App.

Appendix 2:
Prayer: Talking with God

Most Americans say they pray, but not as many pray the way Jesus did and taught His disciples to pray. Fewer, still, really know the power in prayer that God gave us to impact our families, communities, nation, and world. But prayer is our lifeline to God, our means of communicating with our heavenly Father. It develops our relationship—our friendship, fellowship, and intimacy—with Him. In prayer we experience God and are "filled with the Spirit" (Eph. 5:18–21). God uses the prayers of faithful men, women, boys, and girls to heal broken lives and strengthen families, churches, communities, and even nations. He uses our prayers to advance His kingdom on earth (Daniel 9; Acts 4:36)! He wants to so use all believers!

The Essence of Prayer

Prayer is simply talking with God—about anything and everything. He is our Maker, Father, Savior, Provider, and Counselor, our Master, Healer, Guide, and Friend. Christ died for our sins and rose from the dead to sit at the right hand of God the Father, where He is praying for us right now (Heb. 10:12). His Spirit now lives within us and helps us to pray (1 John 4:16).

The Priority of Prayer

Jesus spent time alone with God regularly drawing strength from the Father and seeking His will for every decision (Luke 6:12–13; 22:39–44). His disciples asked Jesus to teach them how to pray (Luke 11:1–13). The apostles knew that prayer and obedience were the keys to Christ's life and ministry and were determined to follow His example: "[W]e will devote ourselves to prayer and to the ministry of the word" (Acts 6:4 ESV). Too few American men pray today, even pastors and leaders! Yet strong praying men are the norm in Scripture. Our families, churches, and nation need men who will make prayer a priority today! (1 Tim. 2:8)

The Practice of Prayer

Scripture teaches, "Pray continually!" (1 Thess. 5:17 NIV); "Praying always" (Eph. 6:18); "Always pray and not give up" (Luke 18:1 NIV). Below are some helps to get you started. No one can beat the Lord's Prayer. It is an outline of key themes to guide our prayer lives:

> "Our Father in heaven,
> hallowed be your name.
> Your kingdom come,
> your will be done,
>   on earth as it is in heaven.
> Give us this day our daily bread,
> and forgive us our debts,
>   as we also have forgiven our debtors.
> And lead us not into temptation,
>   but deliver us from evil." (Matt. 6:9–13 ESV)

In the book of Psalms and throughout Scripture, God has sprinkled prayers: patterns for us to learn from. Here is a simple, popular acronym to help jog our memories:

P-R-A-Y:

- *Praise:* Our Father in heaven, hallowed be your name.
- *Repent:* And forgive us our debts, as we also have forgiven our debtors.
- *Ask:* Give us this day our daily bread, and forgive us our debts, as we also have forgiven our debtors. And lead us not into temptation, but deliver us from evil.
- *Yield:* Your kingdom come, your will be done, on earth as it is in heaven.

Praying Through Scripture

God also talks to us. The Bible is His Word (2 Tim. 2:15; 3:16). Bible in hand, we should pray God's promises back to Him, and claim them for our families, our work, our finances, and our nation (1 Tim. 2:1–8; 1 John 5:14–15).

Scriptures to Pray as a Man: Joshua 1:8; 1 Timothy 3:1–15; 1 Chronicles 12:32; 1 Timothy 6:1–12; 1 Corinthians 16:13; Romans 12:1–21; Micah 6:8; John 4:24; Acts 2:38; 1 Kings 2:2; Husbands: Ephesians 5:25–28; Genesis 2:24; 1 Peter 3:7; Ephesians 4:26–27; Matthew 5:32; Proverbs 5:19; 1 Corinthians 6:18; Fathers: Deuteronomy 4:8–10; 11:18–21; Exodus 34:5–8; Psalm 127:3–5; Matthew 7:11; Ephesians 6:4; Proverbs 22:6; Luke 11:11–12; Hebrews 12:5–7

Scriptures to Pray as a Woman: Matthew 22:36–40; Proverbs 31:30; 1 Peter 3:1–3; Ephesians 5:26; Ephesians 4:15, 29; 1 Timothy 3:11; Ephesians 5:22, 24; 1 Peter 3:1–2; Philippians 4:10– 13;

Philippians 2:3–4; Proverbs 31:12; 1 Corinthians 7:34; Titus 2:3–4; Titus 2:4–5; James 1:19; Ephesians 4:32; 1 Corinthians 7:1–5; Luke 2:37; Colossians 4:2; Proverbs 31:27; 1 Timothy 5:14

Scriptures to Pray for Your Children: Matthew 22:36–40; 2 Timothy 3:15; Psalm 97:10, 38:18; Proverbs 8:13; John 17:15, 10:10; Romans 12:9; Psalm 119:71; Hebrews 12:5–6; Daniel 1:17, 20; Proverbs 1:4; James 1:5; Romans 13:1; Ephesians 6:1–3; Hebrews 13:17; Proverbs 1:10–16, 13:20; 2 Corinthians 6:14–17; Deuteronomy 6; 1 Corinthians 6:18–20; Acts 24:16; 1 Timothy 1:19, 4:1–2; Titus 1:15–16; Psalm 23:4; Deuteronomy 10:12; Matthew 28:18–20; Ephesians 1:3, 4:29; Ephesians 1:16–19; Philippians 1:11; Colossians 1:9; Philippians 1:9–10

Developing Personal Prayer Habits

Rise early each day to pray with opened Bible. Daniel prayed three times daily. Pray whenever you can: as you drive, with your wife, with your children at dinner and before bedtime. You cannot pray too much!

Praying Together with Others

Pray with your spouse regularly. Make time for family prayer. Be part of your church prayer meeting or group. Christ said, "My house shall be called a house of prayer." The apostle Paul instructed Pastor Timothy (1 Tim. 2:1–8) to make prayer the first order of the church, saying prayer is key to peace in the nation. There is nothing like a Spirit-led prayer meeting with people who love the Lord! Praying women have been standing in the prayer gap for decades. Every man must set his heart to become a praying man, lead his family in prayer, and be a strong contributor to the corporate prayer life of his church. We must be leaders in praying for our morally and spiritually troubled, divided nation—and for our national leaders. American Christians simply must respond to God's promise: "If My people who are called by My name will humble themselves, and pray and seek My face, and turn from their wicked ways, then I will hear from heaven, and will forgive their sin and heal their land" (2 Chron. 7:14).

Prayer As Warfare

Jesus described the enemy, the devil, as a thief whose mission is "to steal, and to kill, and to destroy" (John 10:10). Demonic forces are at war against everything good in you, your family, your church, your community, America, and every nation (Eph. 6:10–20).

The devil and his minions are out to thwart the kingdom of God and eliminate righteousness wherever he can. He hates God, hates people, and will use spiritually ignorant and deceived men, women, boys, and girls to do his bidding. Men of God today, like the sons of Issachar in ancient Israel, need to understand the times and know what the church and our nation must do (1 Chron. 12:32). We must pull down Satan's strongholds, wrestle for our families, and use Spirit-led prayer and wisdom to help guide our churches and communities to prevail against the evil onslaught against us (2 Cor. 10:3–5). This is the war of the ages and it is real.

Finally, Determine to Become a Person of Prayer

No matter how long you have been a Christian and may have neglected prayer up until now, you can become a person of prayer starting today. If you have missed the mark, it is not too late. Call upon the Lord, ask His help, and proceed with His guidance. *O Lord, make me a praying person; make me a prayer warrior! In Jesus's name, amen!*

Appendix 3:
How to Share Your Faith

Recent polling from Lifeway Research shows that "only 3 in 10 unchurched Americans (29%) say a Christian has ever shared with them one-on-one how a person becomes a Christian."[7]

Even less are successful in helping someone make a decision to follow Christ. Maybe that is why this whole notion of sharing your faith is so intimidating for many. However, it does not have to be. The best place to start is with your story. Some call it a testimony. In a courtroom, testimony is relied on as part of the evidence in a case. As you are telling your story, you are presenting evidence for how Christ has changed your life for the better. If you are speaking with another man about your faith, think in terms of telling your story in three parts:

1. Your life before you became a follower of Christ.
2. Your encounter with Christ and your decision to follow him as your Savior and Lord.
3. Your life since becoming as a follower of Christ.

The great apostle Paul told his faith story numerous times—several of them are recorded in the Bible. You'll notice these same three parts in Acts 22.

1. Life Before Christ

First of all, notice what Paul said about his life before Christ:

> "I am a Jew, born in Tarsus in Cilicia, but brought up in this city, educated at the feet of Gamaliel according to the strict manner of the law of our fathers, being zealous for God as all of you are this day. I persecuted this Way to the death, binding and delivering to prison both men and women, as the high priest and the whole council of elders can bear me witness. From them I received letters to the brothers, and I journeyed toward Damascus to take those also who were there and bring them in bonds to Jerusalem to be punished." (Acts 22:3–5 ESV)

If there was ever a Jew who was steeped in religion, that Jew was Paul. His religious trophy case was filled to overflowing (v. 3). Over in Philippians 3, he pulled out and dusted off several of them. Then he described his radical commitment to his religion to the point of persecuting followers of Christ (vv. 4–5). Take time to write out what you remember about your life before your life-changing encounter with Christ. Be brief and to the point:

2. Encounter with Christ

Paul not only told about his life before Christ, but then he shared his life-changing encounter with Christ:

> "As I was on my way and drew near to Damascus, about noon a great light from heaven suddenly shone around me. And I fell to the ground and heard a voice saying to me, 'Saul, Saul, why are you persecuting me?' And I answered, 'Who are you, Lord?' And he said to me, 'I am Jesus of Nazareth, whom you are persecuting.' Now those who were with me saw the light but did not understand the voice of the one who was speaking to me." (Acts 22:6–9 ESV)

Notice Paul said in verse 9: "Who are you, Lord?" He was told by a heavenly voice: "I am Jesus of Nazareth, whom you are persecuting." What an amazing encounter! Obviously, most people don't get blinded by a light or hear voices from heaven. However, your story of your encounter with Christ is unique, and no doubt it was (and hopefully still is) a powerful experience for you. Take time to write out your encounter with Christ and how you came to make the decision to follow him as Savior and Lord, but don't rush it. Tell what happened in detail:

3. Life-Change After Christ

Paul then began to tell about the changes in his life after his encounter with Christ:

> "And I said, 'What shall I do, Lord?' And the Lord said to me, 'Rise, and go into Damascus, and there you will be told all that is appointed for you to do.' And since I could not see because of the brightness of that light, I was led by the hand by those who were with me, and came into Damascus.
>
> "And one Ananias, a devout man according to the law, well spoken of by all the Jews who lived there, came to me,

> and standing by me said to me, 'Brother Saul, receive your sight.' And at that very hour I received my sight and saw him. And he said, 'The God of our fathers appointed you to know his will, to see the Righteous One and to hear a voice from his mouth; for you will be a witness for him to everyone of what you have seen and heard. And now why do you wait? Rise and be baptized and wash away your sins, calling on his name.'" (Acts 22:10–16 ESV)

In verse 10, Paul asked, basically, "Lord, what next?" and the risen Christ told him, "You will be told all that is appointed for you to do." And then Ananias, another disciple of Jesus, communicated Paul's assignment in verses 13–16, which was basically to give his testimony and tell his story "to all people." Obviously, Paul accepted his assignment and went on to become one of the greatest leaders in the history of the Christian faith, going on missionary journeys, leading multitudes to faith in Jesus, planting churches, ordaining leaders, even giving his testimony to officials in Rome, which was the capital of the ancient world. He also experienced persecution, imprisonment, and finally death for his faith. Again, Paul's story can be intimidating, but it doesn't need to be. Just think about how your life has changed since you began following Christ. Write down some of your thoughts. Remember, you are trying to offer compelling evidence.

Having read how Paul told his faith story, use the outline above and write out yours. Once you have written it, read through it and prayerfully edit it. After you feel good about it, practice sharing it with another trusted and seasoned believer, preferably someone who has successfully helped lead someone else to faith in Christ. Then you may want to go back and edit it again as you may have thought about a better way to communicate it. Finally, pray for God to open a door of opportunity to share your faith story with someone. Pray that the Holy Spirit will prepare the way for you and do only what He can do. At the end of our best efforts to share Christ, it is still up to God and the individual.

Appendix 4:
The Solution to Our Greatest Challenge

What is the greatest challenge facing families and the church today? It is a lack of a biblical worldview. A worldview is the lens through which we view life and the world around us. Having a biblical worldview means the Bible is our lens. Everything in life is filtered through and viewed from a biblical perspective. The problem is that very few can truthfully claim that the Bible is their authoritative point of reference for what they value and how they behave. In fact, renowned researcher Dr. George Barna has found through extensive surveys measuring against seven core principles foundational to a biblical worldview that only 4 percent of Americans actually view their world through a biblical lens.[8]

What complicates matters is that our worldview is largely developed during childhood. Dr. Barna, Senior Research Fellow for the Center for Biblical Worldview at Family Research Council, has determined that a person's worldview is primarily established between the ages of fifteen months and thirteen years.[9] The problem is that the vast majority of kids reach their teenage years without a biblical worldview.

Here is more definitive evidence. The Nehemiah Institute, founded in 1986, is on a mission to provide worldview assessment to youth in Christian homes associated with Christian schools, homeschool associations, and church youth groups.[10] Called "PEERS," it is the only professionally validated worldview assessment available that I'm aware of. It's fairly comprehensive with seventy test items, fourteen in each category, that the kids take, and it breaks down the results. All the students who take the test fall into four broad categories of worldview:

- Biblical Theism (meaning a Biblical Worldview)
- Moderate Christian
- Secular Humanism
- Socialism

Keep in mind that this is only self-described Christian kids in Christian schools, youth groups, or homeschool. Based on almost forty years of results, PEERS testing shows that a majority of youth from Christian homes are abandoning a biblical worldview and biblical theism in favor of a secular worldview, if not a socialist worldview. When PEERS was first launched in the 1980s, the majority of youth from Christian homes scored mainly in either the moderate Christian worldview or biblical theism worldview. Today, the same demographic shows more than 90 percent of Christian youth scoring in the secular humanism category using the exact same questions that were used in the 1980s, and less than 3 percent are scoring in the biblical theism category. Again, these are kids in Christian schools, church youth groups, and homeschool.

Consequently, this is arguably the single greatest problem facing families and the church in America today, and why we must teach our children. We should not be surprised by these numbers when we are outsourcing the education of our children to people who, for the most part, not only don't have a biblical worldview, but many have an antibiblical worldview. This is why Scripture tells parents that we are primarily responsible to talk about God's Word with our children "when you sit in your house, when you walk by the way, when you lie down, and when you rise up" (see Deut. 6:4–9). We should be teaching our children and our grandchildren the Word of God and its application to our world. Yet when we outsource that to someone else, we see sad results. Of course, we must factor in that it is not simply what's happening in a classroom; it is also shaped by what they're listening to, watching, and engaging with on social media, etc. Furthermore, parents cannot give what they don't have. So, if parents don't have a biblical worldview, they cannot give their children a biblical worldview. And you cannot get a biblical worldview unless you are regularly reading the Word of God.

That brings me to the proposed solution. Again, to gain a biblical worldview, a person must be regularly reading and studying and applying the Word of God. That is what spurred me to develop our Stand on the Word Bible Reading Plan. It is a two-year, chronologically prioritized Bible reading plan that takes ten to fifteen minutes a day of reading, six days a week, Monday through Saturday. On Sunday, there's no reading because it's a discussion day for the family, a day to reflect on what we have read over the previous week and share how God is speaking to us.

This Bible reading plan came about a number of years ago when I was looking for a devotional book for our family—something that would allow five children, ranging from two to eighteen years old, to have a conversation. A lot of people send me books and devotionals with an interest in being a guest on *Washington Watch* to talk about their book, so I had a good handle on pretty much everything that was out there. I looked for six months—read them, studied them, went through them myself—and couldn't find anything that I felt would work. Finally, the Holy Spirit said, "Try the Bible."

So, we began with a couple of books from the New Testament, letters of Paul, and then I began to look at how we could take the entire Bible, breaking it up into a two-year reading plan as opposed to a one-year plan. The latter, for most people, becomes like a speed reading course where not much gets absorbed. However, with the two-year plan, everyone can read it in bite-sized chunks, and each day comes with two questions for reflection. The questions also served as an accountability to gauge who in the family was reading the chapters. And wherever I might be in the world, I would set my clock so that at 7 a.m. central time I would text my family the reading for the day and the two associated questions.

Then on Sunday, after lunch, we would have a conversation about the chapters we read that week and how it applies to the world in which we live. Our weekly time together as a family became the highlight of my week. Here is a suggested template for your gathering:

- Opening Prayer – Praise and a brief prayer for spiritual insight and unity.
- Recap – Briefly summarize the chapters covered that week.
- Discussion Questions – Use open-ended, age-appropriate prompts to spark meaningful worldview conversations. Here are some suggestions:
    1. Most meaningful passage that spoke to you personally?
    2. Insights gained about God: Who He is, What He values and expects, How He works?
    3. Applications that we can make from the Word to what is happening in the world?
    4. How would God have you apply His truth to your life personally?
- Action Steps – Encourage each family member to share a personal takeaway or action step for living the truth revealed in God's Word.

- Closing Prayer – Conclude by praising God for how He has revealed Himself, His purposes, and His ways, and by praying for His help in living in the light of His truth and sharing it with others during the week ahead.

For our family, these Sunday gatherings were nearly as meaningful as a church worship service! Now that nearly all of our kids are grown and some are establishing their own families, I pray they will do the same with their children as God gives them. But that was the strategy we used, and God has blessed it.

That Sunday debrief time is a key part of this strategy to develop a biblical worldview. The inspiration for it came about from a trip I took a number of years ago to Israel and attended a Shabbat dinner with a family. I was fascinated with the conversation around the dinner table, talking about the application of God's Word to the world in which we live. And I thought, "You know, that is what's missing, a conversation to help develop a biblical worldview." I had one child who was in college at the time. So, on Sunday we would dissect what they were being taught (because it was a secular college) and equip them to counter those arguments that they were hearing. We were honing her biblical worldview.

The bottom line here is that it is vitally important that we are intentional about cultivating a biblical worldview in our family members as well as with church members. I believe that reading the Bible daily, with a daily touch-of-base about the reading, followed by an extended weekend conversation can provide the solution to the challenge of making sure our families and our churches develop a biblical worldview. I pray you will join us on this Stand on the Word journey through the Bible. Visit frc.org/Bible to sign up or simply download the Stand Firm app.

Notes

1. Donald Guthrie, "The Pastoral Epistles" in *New Testament Introduction* (InterVarsity Press, 1990), 624.

2. See https://www.usdebtclock.org/ for the up-to-date amount.

3.See J. Rendel Harris, "The Cretans Always Liars" in *The Expositor*, 7th series (October 1906), 2.4:305–17.

4. "History of Hymns: 'Onward, Christian Soldiers,'" September 21, 2017, https://www.umcdiscipleship.org/resources/history-of-hymns-onward-christian-soldiers.

5. See e.g., Tacitus, *Annals*, 44.2–5.

6. See John Foxe, *Foxe's Book of Martyrs* (Hendrickson Publishers, 2004), 5.

7. https://research.lifeway.com/2021/09/09/christians-dont-share-faith-with-unchurched-friends/

8. Tracy Munsil, "Barna, CRC: Widespread Worldview Confusion Grows as Americans Redefine God," Arizona Christian University, February 18, 2025, https://www.arizonachristian.edu/2025/02/18/awvi-2025_01_most-americans-believe-in-a-supreme-power-but-not-the-god-of-the-bible/.

9. Tracy Munsil, "Most US Kids Ages 8-12 Lack Biblical 'Cornerstones,' Research Says," Arizona Christian University, October 11, 2023, https://www.arizonachristian.edu/2023/10/11/most-us-kids-ages-8-12-lack-biblical-cornerstones/.

10. https://www.worldviewcheckup.org/.

Other **STAND on the WORD** Study Guides Available from Fidelis Publishing and Family Research Council

Joshua: Finish Strong! ISBN: 9781956454802
Nehemiah: Rebuilding a Nation ISBN: 9781956454468
Jeremiah: Courage in a Cancel Culture ISBN: 9781956454369
Daniel: Visions and Valor ISBN: 9798992418651
Matthew: The King and His Kingdom ISBN: 9798992418682
Ephesians: Keep Standing! ISBN: 9781956454659
Paul's Prison Letters ISBN: 9798999024657

Also from Fidelis Publishing
and Family Research Council

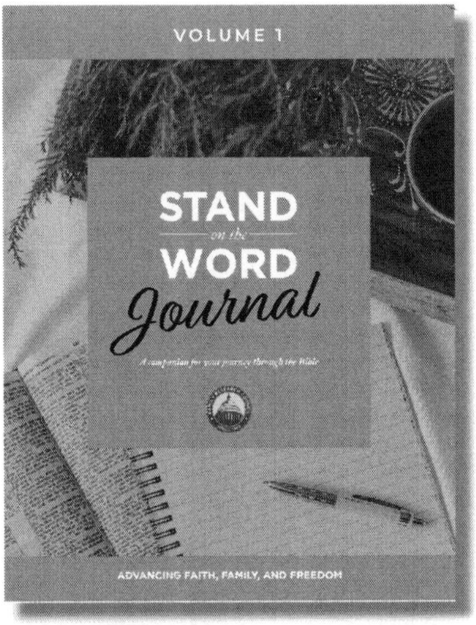

STAND
on the WORD
Journals

Volume 1
ISBN: 9781956454758

Volume 2
ISBN: 9781956454871